Ka

Ragdoll Cats

Everything about Purchase, Nutrition, Health Care, Grooming, Behavior, and Showing

With full-color photographs

Illustrations by
Tana Hakanson Monsalve

BARRON'S

²CONTENTS

HISTORY AND DESCRIPTION OF THE RAGDOLL CAT

Mysterious Hybrid Origins

The Ragdoll cat is a *hybrid* breed, meaning that it did not occur spontaneously in nature, but, instead, was developed through human intervention, the result of years of selectively breeding certain types of cats to achieve a desired product. Although many breeders surmise that the hybridization was achieved by crossbreeding Persian, Birman, and Burmese cats, the Ragdoll's exact origins remain a mystery. The earliest matings took place among mostly feral cats of unknown ancestry; and to complicate matters, some amusing stories that most certainly have been embellished over time lend a fairy-tale air to the breed's lore, making it difficult to separate fact from fiction.

One element of Ragdoll history is certain, however. The late Ann Baker originated the breed in Riverside, California in the early 1960s. Today's Ragdolls can all be traced to the original bloodlines she developed. Baker was reportedly an experienced breeder who raised

Seal point mitted Ragdoll: The Ragdoll is a large heavy-boned cat with long hair, point markings, and blue eyes.

Persian cats, mostly blacks, before she became devoted to developing the Ragdoll cat. Her foundation Ragdoll was a feral, white, long-haired cat of unknown descent named Josephine. Josephine lived among a wild cat colony on the property of Baker's neighbors, the Pennels.

In addition to Josephine's unknown heritage, some colorful tales about her life serve to heighten even more the mystery surrounding the Ragdoll breed. As one story goes, Josephine was struck by a car, and after she recovered from her injuries, the kittens she produced all grew to have the winning traits that would become the hallmarks of the Ragdoll breed. These traits include a large, heavy build, mat-resistant fur, super docility, and nonaggressive dispositions.

A variation of this account holds that Josephine was somehow genetically altered in an experiment at a government facility where she was treated after her accident. Afterward, her kittens allegedly displayed unusual passivity, an insensitivity to pain, and a tendency to go limp in one's arms when held.

While both accounts are generally lumped along with the other amusing myths associated with this breed, the Ragdoll's tendency to go limp when held, likened to picking up a soft bundle of rags or to holding a child's ragdoll toy, is what gives the breed its name. Actually, this tendency to go limp in one's arms may be said of a lot of cats and may be more easily attributed to a docile cat's gentle and trusting nature than to any physical or genetic factor. Other breeds known for their docility, most notably the Persian, are also quite calm and relaxed when held and cuddled by a person they love and trust.

Also, the notion that Ragdolls are insensitive to pain is another myth that has since been dispelled by breeders. Should you accidentally step on a Ragdoll's tail, it will most certainly yowl as loudly as any other cat.

From a scientific standpoint, it is highly unlikely that Josephine's genetic makeup could have changed as a result of her accident, or that any type of genetic experimentation performed during the 1960s could have brought about such a change. Instead, it is more plausible to assume that Josephine simply possessed from birth some remarkable genes of her own that, when coupled with the right mates that could enhance her latent qualities, produced some outstanding offspring. Regardless of how it all really came about, Baker recognized the potential in Josephine's progeny and set out to establish a new breed by selectively breeding Josephine's kittens.

"Sacred Cat of Burma" Look

The original cats Baker used to begin the breed—Daddy War Bucks, Buckwheat, Fugianna, and Tiki—were all related to Josephine, and subsequent generations can be traced back to them. In her writings, Baker generally attrib-utes the Ragdoll's docile temperament to Josephine, but she credits Daddy War Bucks, Josephine's son, as being the father of the Ragdoll look. This cat had dark-colored markings, called *points,* on his face, ears, tail, and front legs, and white mittens on his feet, an appearance that Baker frequently referred to in her writings as the *Sacred Cat of Burma look.* While not a purebred, Daddy War Bucks resembled a Birman cat, a modern-day recognized breed that is often called the Sacred Cat of Burma. Apparently, this look is what inspired Baker to develop the breed.

While Baker occasionally alludes in her writings to the sire of Daddy War Bucks as also having the Sacred Cat of Burma look, the documentation on this issue is unclear. Different accounts suggest that the father of Daddy War Bucks was never seen or known, so the true sire that participated in this tryst with Josephine remains a matter of speculation. As a result, the breed's lineage beyond this point cannot be confirmed with certainty.

To protect her interests in the breed, Baker took an unusual step in the world of purebred cats: She franchised and trademarked the Ragdoll name, and, in return, she collected a royalty fee for every kitten sold by the breeders who contracted with her program.

The Ragdoll Registry

Baker also started her own registry for Ragdolls called the International Ragdoll Cat Association (IRCA). Soon, others began to share her interest in the breed; however, Baker restricted breeding and did not encourage IRCA Ragdolls to be registered with the traditional cat associations. This effectively prevented breeders from being able to exhibit their cats in shows sponsored by the traditional cat associations. Some breeders became dissatisfied with this arrangement and decided to split from her group and form their own alliances.

As a result, the Ragdoll Society was formed in 1975 to promote the breed among the traditional *cat fancy*—a collective term for those who breed and show purebred cats. A few years later, the name changed to the Ragdoll Fanciers' Club. A major goal was to gain recognition for the Ragdoll in the traditional cat-registering associations so that the breed could be more widely shown. Denny Dayton, who, as the club's originator, became instrumental in the Ragdoll's history and acceptance, served as the organization's first president from 1975 to 1978 and as Chairman of the Board from 1979 to 1987. In 1993, the breed club updated its name again to the current Ragdoll Fanciers' Club International (RFCI), which reflects the growing interest of breeders in Japan and other nations.

Today, there are IRCA Ragdolls and non-IRCA Ragdolls on the market. Baker died in 1997, but the Ragdoll trademark and IRCA remain active. IRCA membership has dwindled drastically over the years, and only a handful of Ragdoll breeders remain aligned with this registry. Because IRCA breeders are not allowed to register their cats with any other cat registry, the organization continues to function outside the traditional cat fancy. Of the two organizations, the RFCI is the larger one in existence today, offering insight and information into the welfare and breeding of Ragdoll cats. For addresses of the breed clubs and cat associations, please see Information in the back of this book (page 92).

Achieving Recognition

Ann Baker did register some of her early Ragdolls with the National Cat Fanciers' Association (NCFA), but that was as far as she took the quest for breed recognition among the cat fancy. Although the NCFA was the first traditional association to recognize the Ragdoll as a pure breed, the organization soon ceased operation for a period of time before later reorganizing in 1991.

Meanwhile, Dayton and other breeders who had split away from IRCA campaigned hard to get the breed recognized by The International Cat Association (TICA). In time, they and other interested fanciers successfully advanced their non-IRCA-registered Ragdolls to championship status in TICA, as well as with every other traditional cat association in North America, *except* the Cat Fanciers' Association (CFA).

Advancing to Championship Status

Achieving championship status with a cat-registering association means that the Ragdoll can compete in championship classes and earn points toward titles in shows sponsored by that association. Practices regarding the acceptance of a new breed, or a new variety of an existing breed, vary from one cat-registering association to another. In general, a new breed must meet certain criteria before it achieves full recognition. Typically, a specified number of the cats have to be registered with the association first and shown for a period of time in the *miscellaneous* class, or under *provisional* status, before the breed becomes eligible for scoring awards and titles in championship competition. Depending on the association, the provisional class is also called the *New Breed and Color*, or NBC, class or category.

Tortie point Ragdoll.

Bicolors have points overlayed with white and an inverted "V" on the face.

CFA, the world's largest registry of purebred cats, belatedly accepted the Ragdoll for registration in 1993. The breed advanced through the miscellaneous class and achieved provisional status with that association in February 1998. As noted, provisional status means that Ragdolls can be registered with CFA, but they are not eligible to compete for awards and titles in championship classes. Provisional status in CFA typically lasts about one year before the breed becomes eligible to advance to full championship status. This means that Ragdoll fanciers may reapply for championship status in February 1999. If the application is accepted, Ragdolls could be eligible for championship competition effective with the CFA show season starting May 1, 1999.

For a list of cat-registering associations, see Information in the back of this book (page 92). These associations not only register cats, they also verify the pedigrees and set rules for breeding and showing. The pedigree of a purebred cat lists several generations of its recorded ancestors. In addition to maintaining stud books, the traditional associations sanction shows, present awards, charter clubs, train judges, and approve breed standards.

A *breed standard* is a written guide or definition that describes in detail what the ideal Ragdoll should look like. The Ragdoll Fanciers' Club

The Ragdoll comes in three basic patterns— bicolor, mitted, and colorpoint.

International has a general breed standard for the Ragdoll cat. But each cat-registering association also has its own version. In shows, cats are judged according to how closely they meet the written standard. While the standards may vary in wording from one association to another, and from country to country, they are relatively consistent in their general descriptions that the ideal Ragdoll is a large, heavy-boned cat with long hair, point markings, and blue eyes.

Ragdoll Temperament

Ragdolls make ideal house or apartment companions because they are gentle, quiet, and serene. Their sweet-natured, nonaggressive, laid-back personalities are similar to the Persian's docile disposition. Yet, the Ragdoll's medium to long coat has a plush, silky, mat-resistant texture that doesn't require the daily grooming commitment that a Persian demands. They are easygoing and amiable around children and dogs, and they seem to adapt readily to changes in their surroundings. Quiet and calm, yet moderately active and playful, they prefer interactive play with their favorite human. Ragdolls thrive on human companionship and usually develop strong attachments to their owners.

Loyal and affectionate, Ragdolls often select one human in the household as their preferred companion and will follow that person from room to room, just to oversee the goings-on. Also to this person goes the supreme honor of serving as "the lap" for the cat when the family relaxes in front of the TV. But of course, when the favorite person isn't available, any lap will usually do.

Because Ragdolls have had some of the wilder feline aggressive tendencies and fighting instincts bred out of them, they should be kept strictly indoors and out of harm's way. Despite their feral beginnings, their docile, passive nature makes them unsuitable for life outdoors. But a mild-mannered, gentle, easygoing temperament doesn't mean these cats won't fight back, if necessary. On the contrary, they will defend themselves when they feel threatened.

Although their quiet, passive nature makes Ragdolls well suited to being house or apartment cats, they still need opportunities for play and exercise to stay in shape and to keep from becoming fat. Being highly people-oriented cats, they take special delight in spending time with and being near their owners. So, when you acquire a Ragdoll, make sure you can spend some quality one-on-one time playing with and petting your feline companion. Also, when you acquire a Ragdoll, consider investing in several cat toys and a carpeted cat tree to encourage climbing and playing. Better still, why not get two cats, so they can romp and play with each other!

Colors and Patterns

All Ragdolls are pointed cats, with darker color marking on the ears, face, legs, and tail. The points may be overlaid with white in the bicolor or mitted patterns.

Standard Colors

The Ragdoll commonly comes in four traditional pointed colors—seal point, blue point,

chocolate point, and lilac point. A seal point's body or *ground* color may range from fawn to cream to warm brown. The contrasting points on the ears, face, legs, and tail are a deep seal brown. The blue point's body color is ivory or bluish white with slate blue or silvery blue-gray points. The chocolate point is ivory- or cream-colored with points the shade of light milk chocolate. The lilac point, sometimes called a *frost*, is a lovely milky white ground color with frosty-gray lilac or pinkish-beige points.

Basic Patterns

In addition to the four standard colors, the Ragdoll also commonly comes in three basic patterns—colorpoint, mitted, and bicolor. The colorpoint or *solid* pattern has no white, whereas, the mitted and bicolor patterns overlay the darker point markings with white. Mitted Ragdolls have points on the face, ears, and legs with white *mittens* on the front feet and white *boots* on the hind legs. Bicolors bear points on the ears and tail, but they sport even more white with an inverted "V" extending from the muzzle upward into the darker-colored mask on the face, plus white on the legs, feet, ruff (chin and chest area), and belly.

Other Colors and Patterns

Besides the standard colors and basic patterns, the various cat associations recognize many others, and more colors may be accepted over time. For example, the CFA's provisional standard accepts the Van pattern, in which point markings are restricted to the ears, tail, and upper face. This standard also lists cinnamon point, fawn point, red point, and cream point in all patterns among its accepted colors. The newly developed *lynx* colorpoint pattern, which adds a striking striped effect to the colorpoint areas on the face, legs, and tail, is also included. Breed standards and color descriptions are generally available from the various associations on the Internet or by writing to the organization. Refer to the list of cat registries in the back of this book (page 92).

The Pointed Gene

The gene that gives the Ragdoll its darker points on the extremities is commonly known as the *pointed* gene, but is also called the *Siamese* gene, the *Himalayan* gene, or the Siamese/Himalayan albinism factor. Several other cat breeds have this gene as well, including the Balinese, the Birman and, of course, the Siamese, and the Himalayan. The Himalayan rabbit also sports the same pointed pattern. The pointed gene is linked with another trait that produces blue eye color.

Interestingly, pointed kittens are born looking nearly white. Their points gradually darken with age. Cooler temperatures influence the pigmentation and darkening process as well, which, experts say, explains why kittens remain light colored until they exit their mother's warm womb. After birth, the extremities normally stay a degree or two cooler than the body's core, so these furthermost points tend to darken more.

The RagaMuffin

The RagaMuffin is now recognized as a separate breed in some of the traditional cat associations. Like Ragdolls, RagaMuffins are direct descendants of Josephine, the founding queen of Ann Baker's original IRCA Ragdoll lines. For 30 years, the cats that would become known as RagaMuffins were bred in isolation as IRCA Ragdolls and never exhibited to the public in cat shows.

In 1994, another group of breeders elected to leave the IRCA. Because of the valid trademark on the Ragdoll name, however, this group decided to change the name of their breed from *Ragdoll* to *RagaMuffin*. Today, RagaMuffins are accepted for registration by some of the North American associations, including the American Cat Fanciers Association (ACFA), the United Feline Organization (UFO), and the Cat Fancier's Federation (CFF). The National Cat Fanciers' Association (NCFA) also recognizes the RagaMuffin in all colors and patterns.

Owing to their identical backgrounds, RagaMuffins are similar to Ragdolls in many ways. They are large in size with the same type of plush, medium-to-long-length easy-care coat. They possess the same docile, easygoing temperament, and they demonstrate the Ragdoll's hallmark ability to go completely limp when held in one's arms.

A major difference in the two breeds is the range of recognized colors. While Ragdolls are blue-eyed colorpoints, RagaMuffins are recognized in many more colors, including the spectrum of solids, tabbies, tortoiseshells, and shaded varieties generally associated with the Persian cat. Although colorpoint RagaMuffins are supposed to have blue eyes, the solids and other varieties may have green, gold, or copper-colored eyes.

The original IRCA Ragdoll cats were not all colorpoints. Baker registered the solids and other colors without blue eyes as *Miracle* Ragdolls and continued to use them in her breeding program. Today's RagaMuffin breeders carry on the noble belief that the non-colorpoints are as worthy of preserving and promoting as the colorpoints.

ACQUIRING YOUR RAGDOLL CAT

Before You Buy

Although random-bred "alley" cats make just as good companions as purebred felines, acquiring a purebred Ragdoll has some special advantages. Because a purebred has a recorded ancestry, certain inherited qualities—such as the lovely colorpoint appearance and the laid-back temperament of the Ragdoll—are more predictable. But as you consider getting a Ragdoll, or any cat, remember that your new relationship could last at least a decade or longer. For greatest compatibility, the cat you select as your long-term friend must suit your personality and lifestyle. Before you commit, know what you want in a cat companion. To help you decide, consider the following questions.

One Cat or Two?

Like people, cats can become bored and lonely when forced to stay alone all day while you are away at work. One way to avoid this problem is to get two kittens at the same time, and at about the same age, so they can bond as friends and keep each other company. But if buying two Ragdolls takes too big a bite out of your budget, why not purchase one purebred and adopt a second feline companion from your

Two's company: If you can afford it, buy two Ragdolls, or adopt a second mixed-breed cat from a shelter.

local animal shelter? Mixed-breed cats make excellent pets as well as suitable companions for Ragdolls. Despite their aloof, solitary reputation, cats are highly social animals, and cat acquaintances clearly enjoy each other's companionship.

Male or Female?

Unless you intend to become a breeder, the sex of the cat you choose as your companion should not matter. Both male and female Ragdolls make equally fine companions.

How can you tell whether a kitten is a male or a female? Raise the tail and look at the rear end. In the female, the genital opening looks like a small slit and appears directly below the anus. In the male, the anus and penis are spaced farther apart, and both openings are round.

What About Spaying and Neutering?

If you have no interest in becoming a professional breeder, you definitely will want to spay or neuter your Ragdoll companion when it reaches the appropriate age. Veterinarians traditionally recommend that males be neutered between eight and ten months of age and that females be spayed at six months. But the surgery can now be performed safely at a much earlier age. In fact, to ensure that indiscriminate breeding does not happen, some breeders may elect to spay or neuter their pet-quality purebred kittens early, *before* they sell

*In females (right), the genital opening
appears as a small slit below the round
opening that is the anus. In males (left), the
genital opening is round, with more space
between it and the anus.*

Neutering the male reduces aggressive
behaviors, eliminates testicular diseases, and
decreases the chance of prostate cancer later in
life as well as diseases in other glands affected
by male hormones. Neutering also helps curb
the male cat's bothersome tendency to spray
urine in the house to mark his territory.

Adult Cat or Kitten?

Kittens are cute and adorable, and few people want to miss the joys of this short-lived
stage. However, adult cats often cost less to
acquire than kittens, simply because it is harder
to sell them and find good homes for them.
Typically, breeders keep so many cats in their
catteries that they cannot afford to retain individuals that have been retired from breeding or
showing. The reasonable solution is to place
these retirees in good homes by selling them
for less than the price of a kitten. In most
cases, cats placed in this way are altered and
up-to-date on their annual vaccinations prior
to sale, saving the buyer these initial expenses.

Certainly, kittenhood holds special joys for
cat lovers, but this stage can also be the most
destructive. Kittens are not born knowing how
you expect them to behave in your home. They
have to be properly socialized and patiently
taught not to climb your draperies and not to
sharpen their claws on your couch.

On the other hand, many adult cats are surrendered for adoption because of behavior

them. Studies suggest that the practice of early
spaying and neutering appears to be safe and
does not adversely affect feline maturity, as
was once thought.

Spaying a female cat costs more because
the operation involves opening the abdomen to
remove the ovaries, tubes, and uterus. Remember, however, that the one-time cost of spaying
a female is still considerably less than the long-
term cost of raising and finding homes for suc-
cessive litters of kittens.

Spaying eliminates the female's annoying
heat periods along with her ability to become
pregnant. The operation also eliminates the
possibility of any disease or infections in the
organs removed and decreases the chance that
breast cancer will occur later in life.

Neutering the male cat is a less invasive
procedure that involves removing the testicles.
Both surgical procedures require anesthesia,
but the post-operative, in-hospital recovery
period is generally shorter for males than for
females.

Spaying removes a female cat's ovaries, tubes, and uterus so that she cannot have kittens.

problems related to their past care or to a lack of proper socialization and training. House-soiling and destructive clawing are two of the most common behavior problems that result in cats being surrendered to animal shelters for adoption. In most cases, all you have to rely on is the seller's word and reputation, so ask questions and do your homework!

Indoor or Outdoor Cat?

If you want an outdoor cat, the Ragdoll is not the best breed for you. Because of their passive natures, Ragdolls are better suited to being indoor cats. Breeders of all types of purebreds, not just Ragdolls, often stipulate in their sales contracts that their cats must be kept indoors and allowed outside only with supervision. Still, some people insist on letting their cats roam freely because they believe that depriving cats of their outdoor freedom is cruel.

On the contrary, cats kept indoors live longer, healthier lives. Cats that live their lives totally indoors are less likely to be exposed to diseases, plagued by parasites, hit by cars, attacked by dogs, bitten by wild animals, caught in wild animal traps, poisoned by pesticides, and harmed by cruel people.

You can also expect to have fewer veterinary bills related to injuries from cat fights and similar mishaps if you keep your Ragdoll indoors.

Neutering a male cat renders him unable to sire kittens. The operation also helps reduce or eliminate undesirable spraying behaviors and decreases the chance of prostate cancer later in life.

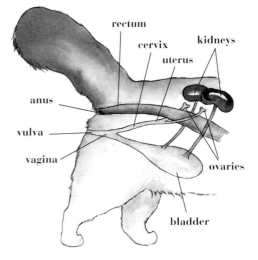

In addition, you will have peace of mind, knowing that your well-cared-for indoor cat has a smaller chance of contracting illness or parasites, such as Lyme disease-carrying ticks, that could affect you or your family.

As long as you provide love and attention, your Ragdoll will be quite happy and well

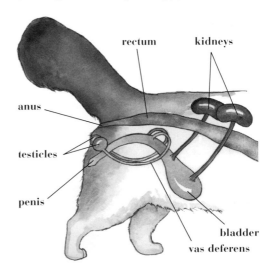

Seal bicolor with white "V" extending upward into the darker mask on the face.

adjusted living indoors. If you feel your Ragdoll *must* experience the outdoors, supervise outings in the yard, build an outdoor exercise run, or install a cat flap that provides safe access to a screened-in porch.

Lifestyle Considerations

Care and Commitment

By now, you realize that acquiring a cat should never be an impulse decision. Acquiring any cat deserves a commitment on your part to take care of the animal's needs from kittenhood through old age. With modern veterinary care and good nutrition, more cats are living longer, an average 15 to 20 years. So, look ahead into your own future and ask yourself if you will be willing and able to provide your Ragdoll with shelter, food, and regular veterinary care for a decade or two.

Housing

Make sure, too, that your housing situation is suitable for owning a cat. If you rent, your landlord may prohibit pets or require an additional fee, plus a pet damage deposit. Remember, as a cat owner, you are liable and responsible for any property damage or personal injuries your animal may cause.

Travel and Time Spent Away

Animals, like children, need special attention and someone to look after them when you're not around. So, before acquiring a cat, consider how much time you normally spend away from home. If you travel often, do you have a trusted friend or relative who will care for your Ragdoll while you're away? If not, can you afford to board your cat or hire a pet-sitter while you're away?

Allergies

Many people are allergic to cats, and unfortunately, many cats are surrendered to animal

Lynx point Ragdoll with distinct stripes on the face.

Ragdoll kittens are priced according to whether they are pet-quality, breeder-quality, or show-quality.

shelters each year because their allergic owners cannot tolerate the severity of their allergy symptoms. So, as you consider getting a Ragdoll, or any cat, think about the people close to you who may become uncomfortable living in or visiting your home because their asthma or allergies worsen in the presence of felines.

Your Age and Health

Certainly, most people expect to outlive their pets, but this is not guaranteed. Consider what would happen to your Ragdoll if you died suddenly or became incapacitated by an injury or illness. Too often, an animal faces neglect, abuse, or abandonment if the owner has not planned ahead for its care in case of an emergency. This is especially true for pet owners who live alone. Give a trusted person advance instructions—and keys—to enter your property immediately and assume care of your Ragdoll if you should die suddenly or become disabled. Talk to a lawyer about providing for your cat's care in your will.

Find a Reputable Breeder

To begin your search for a reputable breeder, call the various cat registries and ask for a list of Ragdoll breeders in or near your area. Read the ads and breeder directories published in the cat trade magazines. Serious breeders also show their cats, so attending cat shows is an especially good way to meet reputable Ragdoll breeders. Visiting a show allows you the opportunity to talk to breeders in person and see firsthand the quality of their cats.

Generally speaking, small-volume breeders are a good source to buy from. When you buy from a private breeder's cattery, you have the advantage of seeing what the dam (the mother), and sometimes the sire (the father), of your kitten looks like. Usually there are other cats present from the same bloodline to give you a good idea of what your kitten's appearance and temperament will be like when it is grown. Also, when you buy from a small-volume breeder, you have the opportunity to establish a relationship with someone who can share his or her experiences in raising and showing Ragdolls.

With the growing number of Ragdoll breeders in the United States, finding one within reasonable driving distance of your home should not be too difficult. However, if the nearest cattery is too far away for you to visit in person, ask to see pictures of the kitten and its sire and dam. Some breeders have computer Web sites and can e-mail you pictures of their cats. Ask for references also; then call other people who've purchased the breeder's cats in the past and find out how satisfied they are with their animals.

If the cattery location is within driving distance, pay a visit. The facility should be clean and free of pungent animal odors. Note whether the cats are kept in cages or allowed to run about freely in an area of the house. While it is not unusual for breeders to keep their studs caged or to confine kittens for their own safety when unattended, it is preferable to acquire a kitten that has been allowed some time to explore its surroundings and socialize with people and other cats.

How Purebreds Are Priced

Breeders price and sell Ragdolls according to whether they are pet-quality, breeder-quality, show-quality, or *top* show-quality. Cats in each category are purebred and fully registrable in the cat associations.

Pet-Quality

Pet-quality Ragdolls are the most affordable. If you have no real interest in showing or breeding Ragdolls, a pet-quality Ragdoll is your smartest buy. You can reasonably expect to pay a minimum of $300 for a pet-quality Ragdoll, maybe more, depending on availability and geographic location. Pricing also can vary widely depending on the kitten's bloodline, type, color, pattern, and markings. Because Ragdolls with mitted feet and a white blaze on the face are in greater demand, they are generally more expensive.

The pet-quality designation in no way means that the cat or kitten is less healthy or less desirable to own than a show-quality animal. It simply means that, in the breeder's opinion, some minor cosmetic flaw—such as too much white or a misplaced marking—makes the cat unsuitable for show ring competition. Generally speaking, only judges, breeders, and other cat fancy enthusiasts familiar with the breed's show standard can tell the difference between a pet-quality Ragdoll and a grand champion.

Responsible breeders will usually sell their pet-quality Ragdoll kittens only with a signed agreement that the new owner will spay or neuter. To ensure that the agreement is honored, the seller may elect to withhold the kitten's papers, or registration slip, until the buyer furnishes a veterinary statement proving that the required operation has been performed. In this way, breeders aim to discourage unethical people from buying purebred cats at pet prices, breeding them for profit, and adding to an already overcrowded pet population.

Breeder-Quality

Breeder-quality Ragdolls also fail to meet the show standard in some small way, yet they possess enough good qualities, in addition to their excellent pedigree, to produce potentially outstanding offspring. Breeder-quality kittens are typically priced in the middle range, selling for somewhat less than their show-quality litter mates, but for more than a pet-quality animal. Expect to pay at least $400 or $500 for a breeder-quality Ragdoll, although pricing can vary widely.

Show-Quality

Show-quality Ragdolls are the most expensive to buy. Expect to pay at least $550 and up, depending on color, bloodlines, and so forth. Breeders consider show-quality kittens to be outstanding examples of the breed, based on the standard, and they anticipate that such kittens will perform well in the show ring.

When shopping for a show-quality Ragdoll, visit a few cat shows where Ragdolls will be exhibited and note who the winners are. Since most exhibitors are breeders, talk to them about your intentions to buy and show, and collect their business cards. If you like a particular color of cat, this is a good way to find out who specializes in what colors. Because breeding good quality Ragdolls is a small-volume business, you may have to put your name on a waiting list as kittens become available, especially if you want a particular color or pattern.

Before buying a kitten for show, carefully study its pedigree. If the kitten comes from a line of champions or grand champions, those cats' names will be prefixed by Ch. or Gr. Ch. The more grand champion titles that appear in the first two or three generations of a kitten's ancestry, the better the chances that the kitten, too, may grow up to be a winner.

Choosing a Healthy Kitten

Once you've found a reputable breeder, the next step is choosing a healthy kitten from the next available litter. The kitten you select should have good muscle tone, bright, clear eyes, and an alert, playful personality. A healthy kitten should not be sneezing or showing mucus discharge around the eyes or nose. The ears should be clean and free of dark, crusty wax. Head-shaking or ear-scratching may indicate ear mites or other infections. The anus should be clean and free of any signs of diarrhea.

The kitten's coat and environment should be clean and free of fleas. To inspect the coat for fleas, rub your hand against the fur and look for fine grains of black dirt, which is really dried flea excrement. Flea signs are more prevalent behind the ears, on the back, and at the tail base, where the kitten cannot easily reach to lick clean.

Tempt the kitten with a feather or ribbon and see how playful and relaxed it is around strangers. If it appears fearful, hisses at you, cringes from your hand, or, in general, seems unused to being handled, look elsewhere for a better socialized kitten.

Once you've selected a kitten, make sure it is certified free of feline leukemia virus (FeLV) and feline immunodeficiency virus (FIV)? Ask for copies of the kitten's health and vaccination records. Have your veterinarian examine it within a day or two after you take it home to help ensure that you've picked a healthy one.

Taking Your Kitten Home

A responsible breeder generally will not let you take home a Ragdoll until it is at least 12 to 16 weeks old. This is because Ragdolls tend to mature more slowly than other breeds, and breeders typically like to keep them longer. By this time, too, a kitten has been weaned and litter-trained, is eating solid food, and has had

most or all of its first year's vaccination series. Besides, kittens that are too young when taken away from their original surroundings some-times suffer from stress and have trouble adjusting to a new environment. Some also may develop unusual behavioral problems related to their maladjustment.

Healthy kittens are playful and inquisitive and should have clear eyes with no nasal discharge.

Ragdoll kittens are born nearly white and gradually darken with age.

Mitted Ragdolls, like this lovely seal point, typically have "mittens" on the front paws and "boots" on the hindlegs.

In addition, if your kitten must be shipped to you, it must be at least three to four months old to conform with most airline age requirements. The breeder usually helps with shipping arrangements, but you can expect to pay all costs, including the airline-approved carrier the kitten will be shipped in. Costs vary, of course, depending on the airline and on the flight distance.

The Sales Agreement

When buying a Ragdoll, always negotiate a written purchase agreement before any money changes hands. A written sales contract describes all terms of the sale, including the purchase price and payment schedule, the breeder's health guarantee, and any neuter/spay requirement. Contracts may vary from breeder to breeder; however, all agreements should spell out the buyer's option to return the kitten and get his or her money back if the kitten is found to be unhealthy or unsuitable within a specified period after purchase.

The breeder's contract also may require the kitten's new owner to give the

Seal bicolor.

breeder the first option to buy back the kitten if the new owner can no longer keep it. Aside from stipulating whether an animal can be used for breeding, breeders may include other provisions in their contracts as well, barring the sale of the kitten to a pet shop or research facility or prohibiting declawing the cat. Be sure you read and agree to the terms in the sales contract.

Health records and vaccination certificates should accompany the sales agreement. To save money, some breeders vaccinate their own kittens, which is a legal practice. However, in areas where rabies shots are required for cats, the vaccine must usually be administered in the presence of a state authority, such as a veterinarian or an animal control officer, before a legal certificate can be issued. When shipping kittens by air, health and rabies certificates are typically required, depending on the destination and on the airline's regulations.

The Registration Form

Registering a kitten enables you to show it in purebred competition classes, if you choose to do so. Whether you intend to show or not, you want to buy a Ragdoll that is registrable. This means that the kitten's pedigree, or family history, can be verified and accepted by the cat-registering associations. With no proof of its parentage, a Ragdoll without papers may not be a purebred. Remember, you are paying for the predictable qualities that a certain bloodline offers. On the other hand, it's important to understand that papers alone do *not* guarantee the health or quality of a kitten.

The purchase price should include the kitten's papers and pedigree; however, the breeder may give you the kitten's registration slip at the time of sale or mail it to you later, depending on the terms of your agreement. For example, if the contract stipulates that the cat cannot be used for breeding, you probably will not receive the kitten's individual registration form until you furnish proof that you've had your kitten spayed or neutered. Without this form, you cannot register your kitten, nor can its future progeny be registered. If the *Not For Breeding* box on the form is checked and signed, the cat-registering association will not allow kittens from that cat to be registered

When you receive the form, simply fill it out with the name you have chosen for your Ragdoll. Complete the owner information section and mail the form with the proper fee(s) to the association(s) in which the breeder registered your kitten's litter. The breeder will have completed the sections about your kitten's breed, sex, hair length, eye color, coat color, and so forth. Also, if the breeder has a cattery name, that name will be printed on the line where you write in the name you choose for your kitten. The cattery name will be part of your kitten's official, registered name. Most forms direct you to select two or three names, in case your first choice has already been used by someone else. When the association receives the form, it will verify the pedigree information, approve your name selection, then send you back an owner's certificate.

To Breed or Not to Breed?

So, now you have your cat, or you've at least made up your mind to purchase a purebred Ragdoll. Most people who develop a serious interest in cats will, at some point, consider going into business as a breeder. Should you?

Probably not. Breeding purebred Ragdoll cats should be undertaken by only the most serious and dedicated cat fancier. It is an expensive and labor-intensive hobby. Stud fees typically start at $250 and go up, depending on the male's quality, color, and show record. If the stud is a grand champion or a national winner, you can count on the fee being significantly higher. Figure in the travel costs of transporting the queen to the stud for breeding, the veterinary bills, vaccinations, cat food, advertising expenses, and so forth, and you can quickly calculate how little a breeder actually profits from raising a litter of kittens.

Even after writing off allowable expenses on their business taxes, most professional breeders consider themselves lucky if they break even. Obviously, if people don't do it for the money, there must be other rewards. To serious breeders, the real profits in breeding are intangible achievements, such as a Best in Show rosette, regional and national awards, and the respect of fellow cat fanciers who recognize their contributions to the Ragdoll breed. If these kinds of goals and rewards do not interest you, leave breeding to the professionals, and have your pet Ragdoll spayed or neutered.

Beware of people who fancy the idea of breeding cats and selling the kittens to make a quick profit. These are *backyard breeders* who know little about feline genetics and even less about the concept of responsible pet ownership. Don't deal with one of these.

Then there are people who have the misguided notion that breeding their cat *just once* will allow their children to learn one of life's profound lessons by witnessing the miracle of birth. Unfortunately, this notion only adds to the pet overpopulation problem, even if you take the time to find good homes for the kittens. The real lesson to teach is how important it is for all of us to take responsibility for the animals already in this world. Instead of breeding more kittens that may end up homeless in shelters, teach kids how proper health care, spaying, and neutering can reduce the suffering that more than eight million surplus, unwanted pets endure each year.

Concentrate instead on being the best-educated cat owner you can be. Share your knowledge with others. Read books about cats. Subscribe to cat magazines. Visit cat shows. Volunteer at your local animal shelter. Set a good example as a responsible cat owner, and others who know you will follow and learn.

BRINGING YOUR RAGDOLL CAT HOME

Pet Supplies

Bringing home a new kitten is an exciting time for the whole family, but the sudden change to new surroundings may be somewhat intimidating from the new arrival's viewpoint. To make your Ragdoll's transition to its new home as comfortable as possible, a little planning and preparation are in order. You'll want to have on hand some basic pet supplies, such as cat food, the day your kitten arrives.

Food and Water Dishes

Every pet in the household should have its own feeding dish, so select one ahead of time for your new Ragdoll and decide on a feeding location. Stainless steel, ceramic stoneware, or glass dishes, although more expensive than plastic feeding bowls, are generally easier to keep clean because they can be sterilized in the dishwasher without melting or warping. Ceramic dishes come in decorative varieties, but select only the ones sold for human use or labeled as lead-free.

Although they are less expensive, plastic dishes tend to develop tiny pits and scratches over time, which can harbor bacteria and

Scratching posts can double as lofty sleeping quarters.

odors, despite diligent cleaning. The stale food odors that collect in these minute crevices may go unnoticed by the human nose, but your cat, with its more highly developed sense of smell, may find the odor buildup offensive enough to refuse to eat. To deter odor buildup, buy plastic dishes that are dishwasher-safe so they can be heat sterilized between meals. Another sound precaution is to replace plastic dishes with new ones periodically.

When selecting feeding dishes, keep in mind that most cats seem to prefer flat, shallow saucers or plates to deep bowls. Apparently, cats dislike having their sensitive whiskers rub the sides of the dish as they eat. In fact, some cats dislike this unpleasant sensation so much that they will resort to scooping out food morsels with their paws and eating off the floor.

Also, choose a weighted food dish that's heavy enough to stay put and not slide across the floor as the cat eats. Imagine how frustrating your meals would be if your plate kept sliding across the table every time you tried to take a bite!

Cat Carriers

To bring your kitten home, you'll need a suitable cat carrier for the animal to travel in safely. You'll use the carrier to cart your cat to veterinarians, boarding facilities, or cat shows, as well. Available at pet supply stores, and sometimes veterinarians' offices, pet carriers range from inexpensive fold-out cardboard boxes to the sturdier molded plastic ones. There are also wicker baskets and canvas totebag varieties. If your Ragdoll must be shipped by air, the airlines will specify the dimensions and type of pet carrier required in the cabin or in the cargo hold. Regardless of the carrier type you select, it should fasten securely and be well ventilated so that the animal inside cannot escape but can get plenty of fresh air.

If you have more than one cat, each animal should have its own carrier for safe transport. Avoid putting two cats together in a single carrier, even if they are best friends. The too-tight quarters and the stress of travel might cause them to fight and injure one another.

Cat Beds

Most cats like to select their own sleeping places and will alternate their napping spots on a whim. More than likely, your Ragdoll's pre-ferred siesta site will probably be *your* bed or your favorite chair. Many people like to share their beds with their cats. However, if you want to discourage your Ragdoll from sleeping with you, keep your bedroom door shut or confine your cat to a certain area of the house during the night.

Regardless of your sleeping arrangements, you should provide your cat with its own bed. Whether you buy a plush, fancy cat "cozy" from the pet store or simply throw an old blanket in a cardboard box, select something washable, because you want to be able to launder your cat's bedding frequently.

Scratching Posts

A sturdy scratching post is another essential piece of equipment for cats confined to the indoors. Cats have an instinctive need to scratch and sharpen their claws on objects in their territory. Even declawed cats continue to display this natural feline behavior. The action not only removes dead nail and recon-ditions the claws but also marks territory with scent from glands in the paw pads. You cannot eliminate the cat's natural instinct to sharpen claws, but you can contain the behavior by providing your Ragdoll with a scratching post.

Pet shops and pet supply catalogs sell scratching posts in many shapes and sizes. Carpeted cat trees that extend from floor to ceiling make attractive scratching posts and come in all colors to match any room's decor. Creative designs incorporate built-in perches and peekaboo penthouses for cat-napping. Not only do they double as lofty sleeping quarters, they offer ample exercise and climb-ing opportunities for indoor cats.

Before introducing your Ragdoll to its scratching post, make sure the post isn't wob-bly and won't tip over as the cat claws it. Obvi-ously, if a flimsy, unstable post falls over and frightens your cat, the animal likely will refuse to go near it ever again, and understandably so. The base must be wide and supportive enough to remain standing and balanced, even when accosted by the full weight of a clawing, jumping, or climbing adult cat.

Introduce your Ragdoll to the scratching post at an early age, or as soon as you bring the newcomer into your home. Simply show the cat the post, move its paws in a scratching motion, and praise lavishly when it does what you want. If necessary, rub some dried catnip on the post to entice your Ragdoll to play and climb on it. If the cat decides to try out your furniture, scold verbally by saying "No" in a loud, sharp tone. Or, squirt jets of clean water from a water pistol to startle the cat without harming it. Wait a few minutes, then carry the cat to its scratching post.

Once clawing the furniture becomes an established habit, it is difficult to break, but not impossible. The recommended strategy is to make the inappropriate surface unattractive to the cat while, at the same time, offering a more appealing, acceptable substitute, such as a suitable scratching post. To discourage an undesirable scratching habit, cover the problem area temporarily with a loosely-draped blanket, newspaper, wrapping paper, plastic bubble wrap, or sheets of aluminum foil. Then, as previously explained, consistently encourage the cat to use the acceptable substitute.

Ragdolls are easy to train and readily learn to respond to voice tones and commands. If you are consistent and persistent in your methods, your cat should soon learn to restrict its clawing to the designated area. When disciplining your cat, use your voice, but never, *never* strike the animal with your hand, with a folded newspaper, or with any other object. Such abusive action will only make your Ragdoll fearful and distrustful of humans.

Litter Boxes

A litter box is essential equipment for any cat that spends time indoors. Pet stores and mail-order catalogs carry a wide variety of litter pans, from the basic open plastic models to the fancy ones with ventilated bottoms and pull-out trays.

Cleanliness: Regardless of the kind of litter pan you select, it's important to keep the box clean, or the cat may stop using it if it becomes too soiled. You'll also need a litter scoop to remove solid wastes from the box daily. Keeping the box clean and changing the litter frequently are the best ways to control litter box odor in your home. A little bit of baking soda sprinkled on and stirred into the litter also helps control odor in close quarters. Or try one of several commercial cat box odor control products available at pet supply and grocery stores.

Location: For privacy, place the litter box in a quiet, undisturbed area of the house. Do not place it too near the cat's food dishes or sleeping quarters. Being fastidious creatures, cats normally do not like to eat or sleep near the place where they relieve themselves.

If you have more than one cat, provide each with its own litter box, and place the pans in separate locations, if necessary. Although cat friends will often share litter pans, some more aggressive cats may chase others away in a show of dominance. Without an alternate box to use, the subordinate cat may have no choice but to use the carpet or some other inappropriate place.

Litter Box Training: By the time your Ragdoll is old enough to leave its mother and go to its new home, it should already know how to use a litter box. The instinctive digging and covering behaviors come naturally to cats, and they learn the rest by observing and imitating their mothers.

Generally, all you have to do is show the kitten where its new litter box is. Do this when you first bring the kitten home and again after the kitten's first few meals in its new surroundings, and it should quickly catch onto the idea.

You'll need a sturdy pet carrier for safe transport to the veterinarian, shows, and any other places you might take your cat.

If the kitten seems slow to catch on, it may be necessary to confine it temporarily to a small area with a litter box, until it does its business. Sometimes adding a single drop of ammonia to the litter helps. The scent of ammonia, being a by-product of urine, usually attracts cats to use the spot as a potty.

Litter Box Fillers: Litter selection is important, because if your cat doesn't like the texture or scent of the type you choose, it may refuse to use the box. Some cats dislike the perfumed or chemically treated pellets added to commercial litters for odor control. These additives may please human noses, but cats seem to prefer their own scent. For really finicky felines, plain, untreated clay litter or sterilized sand may be better choices. Avoid using dirt from the yard or garden, however, as it may contain insect larvae or other unwanted organisms, including the one that causes *toxoplasmosis* (see page 35).

Some litter brands are designed to clump when moistened, making it easier to scoop out clumps of urine along with the solid wastes. This clumping action aids greatly in sanitation and odor control by leaving behind only clean, fresh litter.

Certain clumping brands have an unfortunate tendency to stick to a cat's fur, although many manufacturers have worked to correct

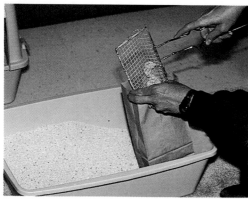

Litter boxes come in a variety of styles, from the covered pans to the basic open plastic types. Keep the litter box clean by scooping out waste every day.

A scratching post is essential equipment for indoor cats.

this problem. So, with a longhaired cat like the Ragdoll, you should inspect the backside and hind legs on occasion to make sure litter is not sticking to your cat's fur.

In addition, concerns have been raised about clumping litters causing digestive blockages, if swallowed. As a precaution, avoid using a clumping litter with young kittens, as they are more likely than adults to sample the stuff by tasting and eating it. Then, when your Ragdoll is grown, switch to a convenient clumping brand if you like.

Most litter brands cannot be flushed down toilets. So, to avoid wrecking your bathroom plumbing, read product labels carefully.

Cat Toys

Indoor cats need toys to play with, but you don't have to spend a lot of money on them. Cats can amuse themselves with ordinary items you might use in your own recreational pursuits, such as Ping-Pong balls, golf balls, and tennis balls. Leftover wrapping paper and paper grocery bags are a great favorite, too, but *never* use plastic bags for this purpose or leave them unattended around your Ragdoll, because cats, like children, may suffocate in them. A cardboard box with cut-out peep holes is another inexpensive toy that can give your cat hours of delight.

Safe toys: When selecting toys at the pet store, consider safety first. Choose only sturdy toys that won't disintegrate after the first few mock attacks. Remove tied-on bells, plastic eyes, button noses, and dangling strings that

your cat could tear off and swallow or choke on during play. Never let your Ragdoll play with small items that could be chewed or swallowed easily, such as buttons, bows, hairpins, rubber bands, wire bread-wrapper ties, paper clips, cellophane, or wadded-up candy wrappers.

Supervise all access to fishing pole-style toys with feathers, sparklers, and tied-on lures. These interactive toys provide great exercise in your watchful presence, but if left unattended, the attached line poses a potential hazard for being

Blue bicolor.

wide range of symptoms, including mouth irritation, drooling, vomiting, diarrhea, hallucinations, convulsions, lethargy, and coma. If your cat displays any unusual behavior after chewing on a plant, consult a veterinarian immediately. The National Animal Poison Control Information Center also offers a comprehensive list of plants toxic to cats. The center's number is listed in the back of this book (see page 92).

◆ **Holiday decorations:** Although accidental poisonings can happen any time of the year, they seem to be more prevalent during the year-end holidays. That's because cats like to investigate and sometimes sample the greenery and decorations commonly used for holiday decorations—poinsettia, holly berries, mistletoe, tinsel, angel hair, and artificial snow. Ingesting these items can be potentially dangerous for cats, so either avoid using them, or restrict your cat's access to the decorated rooms.

Outdoor Hazards

Even though you may have wisely decided to keep your Ragdoll safely indoors, there likely will be times when you will want to allow your cat outside for short periods with supervision. When you do so, be aware that there are many potential hazards as close as your backyard and driveway. Here are some to remember:

◆ **Lawn care products:** Pesticides, weed killers, fungicides, and fertilizers can poison pets that walk in treated areas, then lick the chemicals off their paws. So read lawn care and pesticide product labels carefully before using. Avoid letting your cat outdoors to pad through freshly treated areas until the first rain or the next thorough watering has rinsed away the substance.

◆ **Pools and ponds:** Supervise pets around swimming pools and ponds, just as you

Ragdolls, being highly sociable, generally get along well with other cats and pets in the household.

conta
child
child'
tly st
that I
frigh
like t
the e
that s
their
tolera
trust.
up ar

Cats

Co
they
We've
tales"
mout
wise
acces
truth
a bab
frigh
scrat
door
out o
tent.
nets 1

To
becau
mean
to-be

would a child. Although cats can swim, kittens, especially, can drown from exhaustion if they fall in and can't find a way to climb out of the water.

◆ **Antifreeze leaks:** The driveway is another area where special precautions should be observed. Ethylene glycol, the prime ingredient in traditional antifreeze, is poisonous to animals. As little as half a teaspoon can kill an adult cat. So if your car has even a tiny cooling system leak, you may put your own cat, or your neighbors' pets, at risk. To avoid this, immediately hose down or wipe up all fluid leaks and antifreeze spills, no matter how small. When adding fluids to your car, use a funnel to prevent spills.

Consider replacing your car's traditional antifreeze with a safer antifreeze brand. Safer antifreeze products on the market contain *propylene glycol*, which is significantly less toxic than ethylene glycol. In fact, propylene glycol is used as a preservative in some foods, alcoholic beverages, cosmetics, and pharmaceuticals. Even though your Ragdoll is an indoor cat, using a safer antifreeze is a humane practice that can benefit free-roaming domestic animals and wildlife.

Ragdolls and Other Pets

Ragdolls, being highly sociable and adaptable, generally get along well with other pets. But

Chocolate point Ragdoll: Children must be taught how to hold and handle cats properly.

FEEDING YOUR RAGDOLL CAT

Commercial Cat Foods

Commercial pet foods come in three basic types: canned, semimoist (also called soft-dry), and dry. Each type comes in a variety of flavors as well. While there's no reason to complicate the selection process, there are some advantages and disadvantages of each type of food to consider before you settle on a favorite.

Dry Foods

These are generally less expensive to buy and more convenient to serve. They are not as smelly as canned foods, and they can be left out all day without spoiling for cats to nibble *ad libitum* or at will. Called free-choice feeding, this is the method most often recommended in the product-feeding guidelines on a dry food package label.

Unfortunately, owners often make the mistake of leaving out too much dry food, encouraging their cats to overeat and grow fat. Therefore, instead of putting out bulk amounts of dry food that could last for several days, it is best to carefully measure out each meal or each day's portion, using the product feeding recommendations as a guide. By leaving out only controlled portions of dry food for free-choice nibbling, you are less likely to end up with an obese cat (see page 47).

Kittens need a feline growth formula commercial cat food for their first full year.

At one time, it was thought that letting cats nibble on dry foods throughout the day predisposed them to a lower urinary tract condition called *feline urologic syndrome* (FUS) by allowing the urine pH to become too alkaline. Now, with improved pet food products on the market, reformulated with acidifying ingredients to better maintain urine pH levels within normal acidic ranges, free-choice feeding is no longer the hotly debated issue it once was in this regard.

Dry foods also may benefit cats by promoting better dental health. Although this issue, too, has been widely debated, it is generally believed that the hard chewing action required with dry foods helps scour the teeth and gums, and thus, aids in controlling ugly tartar build-up that can lead to gum disease and tooth loss. Because cats tend to swallow their food almost whole, the benefits of such chewing action are probably minimal at best. So, feeding dry foods should not be considered a substitute for routine dental care.

Canned Foods

Canned foods are usually more expensive than dry foods. They contain more moisture than either dry or semimoist foods, making them a better choice for cats that need more water due to some medical condition, such as kidney disease. For cats that have missing teeth or sore gums due to dental disease, canned foods are also ideal because they require virtually no chewing.

Finicky eaters also seem to prefer canned foods and will often select them over dry foods. This is because most canned foods apparently taste better to the feline consumer. Canned foods typically contain more protein and fat than either dry or semimoist foods, which makes them generally more palatable to the feline taste buds.

Single-serving cans, although more expensive, result in less waste, because many cats will refuse to eat canned food after it has been refrigerated. Having evolved as predators, cats prefer their food warm, at the average body temperature of small prey animals or, at least, at normal room temperature. So always warm refrigerated leftovers before serving. When warming leftovers in the microwave oven, test the portion with your finger before serving to make sure it is not too hot. A cat that burns its mouth on hot food will probably refuse that type or variety the next time.

Canned foods will spoil quickly and attract insects if left out too long, so free-choice feeding is not an option with this type. To avoid spoilage and odors, take up any uneaten portions of canned food as soon as the cat finishes eating.

Semimoist Foods

These foods typically come in soft-dry nuggets packaged in foil-lined wrappers or bags. Semimoist foods attempt to combine some benefits of the dry and canned types, making them an attractive, middle-of-the-road choice for human consumers to use for their cats. Semimoist foods contain more moisture than dry foods, but they lack the odors of canned foods

that human consumers so often find offensive. Also, like dry rations, semimoist foods can be left out and fed free-choice without spoiling. Unlike dry foods, however, semimoist products are too soft to help reduce dental tartar. The convenience packaging is a major advantage, because the single-serving foil pouches take the guesswork out of controlled-portion feeding.

At one time, semimoist cat food products contained a preservative called *propylene glycol*, which is the same chemical used in safer antifreeze brands (see page 33). This chemical also appears in many cosmetics, medicines, and alcoholic beverages used by humans; however, its use is no longer allowed in cat food products, because it has been implicated in causing red blood cell damage in cats.

Popular vs. Premium Brands

Aside from the basic food types, cat foods are also packaged and marketed according to whether they are generic (economy brands), popular, or premium brands. While the cheaper generic foods, which are typically sold under a private label or store name, tend to be lower in quality and use poorer-grade ingredients, this is not always true. Sometimes it is cheaper for a manufacturer to simply stick a generic label on a popular brand and market it under a different name without changing the formula. Before choosing a generic brand, however, you should contact the manufacturer and thoroughly research the product ingredients.

The nationally advertised, popular name-brand products are sold in supermarkets, while the more expensive premium brands are sold primarily through pet supply stores and veterinarians' offices. Other than price, some popular and premium brands may differ very little. There is no industry-regulated definition for what a *premium* or a *super-premium* product should be and no higher nutritional standard that premium pet foods must adhere to. These words are simply descriptive marketing tools.

The general assumption is, however, that premium foods contain higher-quality ingredients and remain stable in their makeup, whereas, popular brands are more likely to change recipe ingredients according to the current market cost and availability of those ingredients.

Premium products also are often marketed as being more digestible and *energy dense,* which means that a smaller amount is required per serving to provide the necessary nutrients. Another general assumption is that the product research behind premium brands is more substantial. However, many well-known popular brands are also backed by extensive research and years of experience on the part of the manufacturer.

Therapeutic diets, often called prescription diets, also are available through veterinarians for cats with special needs. These foods are formulated and dispensed by veterinarians specifically for certain health conditions, such as heart disease, kidney disease, intestinal disorders, or obesity. While most of these special diets come in dry or canned form, at least one for recurrent gastrointestinal problems is available in semimoist form.

Life-Cycle Nutrition

Good nutrition is a relative term that depends a great deal on a cat's age, activity level, and current state of health. What's good for a kitten is not necessarily the best choice for an older

How to Avoid Finicky Behavior

Well-known for their finicky eating habits, cats have a discriminating sense of taste. Once developed, their taste preferences can be difficult to change. A cat fed the same type or flavor of food all its life may steadfastly refuse any sort of dietary change, even if its health depends on it. To avoid creating finicky eating behaviors, and to provide variety and appetite appeal, select two or three high-quality products your Ragdoll seems to like and use them interchangeably. Alternating a few varieties of cat foods and flavors from kittenhood on will go a long way toward preventing your cat from becoming addicted to one type of food.

cat, and vice versa. Research has shown that certain nutrients consumed at too high or too low levels during early life stages may contribute to health problems in later life. This knowledge ended the old womb-to-tomb practice of feeding cats one food their entire lives, and ushered in a new era of life-cycle nutrition.

Today's pet food labels state whether the product is formulated for *growth and reproduction, adult maintenance,* or for *all life stages* of the cat. Most manufacturers make product lines geared to all three.

Growth and reproduction formulas are made specifically to satisfy the extra nutrient requirements of growing kittens and pregnant or nursing queens (female cats). Foods formulated for *all life stages of cats* meet these same requirements because they must satisfy the range of nutritional needs for cats of all ages. However, *adult maintenance* formulas are intended primarily for fully grown, nonbreeding, and generally less active felines. This means that foods

labeled for adult maintenance do not have to meet the higher nutrient requirements of growth and reproduction formulas. For this reason, adult maintenance diets are *not* satisfactory fare for kittens or pregnant cats.

Dry foods can be left out all day for free-choice nibbling, but it is best to provide each cat with its own bowl.

Feeding Kittens

For its first full year, your Ragdoll kitten needs a greater amount of high-quality protein for growth than it will require in adulthood. At least 30 to 40 percent of a kitten's diet should be protein. Select a kitten or feline growth formula designed to meet this extra need. Follow the feeding guidelines on the package, adjusting the portions as needed. In general, you should let growing kittens eat as much as they seem to want.

Bulk feeders and waterers are handy and convenient for times when you need to leave your cat overnight.

Blue bicolor with mitted kitten.

While a high-quality food formulated for *all life stages of cats* is also adequate, dry foods formulated for growth and reproduction are usually molded into smaller morsels that make it easier for smaller mouths to chew. Kittens require more frequent feedings, but in smaller quantities, than adult cats. Newly-weaned kittens need three or four feedings a day. By about age six months, two meals a day should suffice.

Feeding Pregnant Cats

During periods of gestation (pregnancy) and lactation (nursing), breeding females ideally should receive a high-quality food formulated for feline growth and reproduction. Because foods labeled for *all life stages* of cats must meet the same requirements as growth and reproduction formulas, these products are also sufficient. Because of the extra demand placed on their bodies, pregnant and nursing cats need more calories and high-quality protein to aid in fetal development and milk production. Again, follow the feeding guidelines on the package, adjusting the portions as needed. As with growing kittens, you should allow pregnant cats access to as much food as they want to eat.

Feeding Moderately Active Cats

Adult, nonbreeding cats need enough nutrients, fiber, and protein to satisfy their appetites, yet prevent them from getting fat. While a food formulated *for all life stages of cats* may be fine for many adult felines—especially for the very active breeds—some cats tend to become overweight, particularly during middle age. Because Ragdolls tend to be laid back as individuals and moderately active in their adult years, a suitable commercial food formulated for *adult maintenance* may be an appropriate choice, especially if your cat tends to be a little overweight. Your veterinarian can best assess your cat's weight, body condition, and nutritional needs at any given age and recommend an appropriate diet.

Because adult maintenance formulas contain less protein than the growth and reproduction foods, or foods formulated for all life stages, they are unsuitable for growing kittens or pregnant cats. They are, however, adequate for a normal, nonbreeding adult's lower energy requirements.

Feeding Senior Cats

Foods labeled *for all life stages* are designed to meet the needs of all cats, from kittens to senior citizens. However, older, less active cats often require fewer calories, less salt, and less protein than these diets contain. Cats with special health concerns, such as kidney or heart disease, may also require one of several therapeutic diets available through veterinarians.

Still other cats in their advanced years, although in relatively good health, may start getting thin because their bodies are no longer able to digest nutrients from their food as well as when they were young. To maintain their weight and condition, some of these older cats—as long as they're healthy and not suffering from kidney disease or other medical problems—may thrive better on a highly digestible or energy-dense food to help make up for the nutrients their bodies are wasting. In some cases, a high-quality kitten or growth formula

may even be appropriate for an otherwise healthy older cat. Such a choice would *not* be appropriate, however, if your veterinarian determines that your elder cat's kidney function has been compromised by old age or disease. Instead, the veterinarian may recommend a special food with only moderate levels of high-quality protein to ease the burden on the kidneys.

Remember, your veterinarian is the best judge of your Ragdoll's overall condition and dietary needs. Weight loss and other changes in your cat's condition need to be evaluated medically to rule out underlying causes, such as kidney failure or thyroid disease. Cats are generally considered *seniors* at about age ten, but before your Ragdoll reaches the decade mark, ask your veterinarian to reassess your cat's dietary needs and recommend any appropriate changes in feeding rations and routine.

Making Dietary Changes

With so many product lines and varieties to choose from, the important thing to remember is that no one perfect pet food exists for every cat and for every owner. That's why it may be necessary to change foods from time to time, as your cat's nutritional needs vary.

Although pet food labels provide helpful information, choosing a cat food solely by label contents or brand name is unwise. Instead, base your selection on how well your Ragdoll performs and maintains its overall condition on a particular food. Start with a high-quality kitten food that your breeder or veterinarian recommends. Then, during annual checkups, as your veterinarian assesses your Ragdoll's condition, remember to ask about your cat's changing dietary needs as it reaches adulthood and matures into middle and old age.

Make recommended changes to your cat's diet gradually, over a period of at least a week or more. Sudden changes in diet or feeding routine may result in symptoms of gastrointestinal upset in some animals, or your cat may simply refuse to eat the new food. So, begin making any dietary change by mixing small amounts of the new food with your cat's current rations. Gradually increase the amount of new food as you decrease the amount of old food until the changeover is complete.

Deciphering Cat Food Labels

Pet food companies are required by law to supply certain nutritional information on their labels. We have already discussed the life-cycle formulas and what these disclosures on a cat food label mean. A pet food label must also disclose whether the food is formulated to provide complete and balanced nutrition. The word *complete* means the food has all the necessary nutrients a cat needs for good health. The word *balanced* means those necessary nutrients are present in the proper proportions. If the label doesn't say the food is *complete and balanced*, chances are, it isn't.

Statement of nutritional adequacy: To prove that their products comply with nutritional guidelines set forth by the Association of American Feed Control Officials (AAFCO), and to substantiate claims of "100% complete and balanced" nutrition, pet food manufacturers must either adhere to a proven formula or subject their products to lengthy feeding trials with live animals. Of the two, feeding trials offer more assurance that the food is ade-

quately nutritious, because the product has been test-fed to cats for a period of time under AAFCO protocols. Any product that has undergone feeding trials says so on the package. Look for the company's statement of nutritional adequacy, which should say something similar to: *Animal feeding tests using AAFCO procedures substantiate that [this brand name] provides complete and balanced nutrition for the maintenance of adult cats.*

Guaranteed analysis: The required guaranteed analysis must state on the label only whether minimum or maximum amounts of nutrients, in percentages, were met. It doesn't have to list actual concentrations of specific nutrients. The problem with not knowing how much a product exceeds the minimum requirement for a certain nutrient, such as protein, is that sometimes too much can be just as bad as too little, depending on the cat's age and condition. What that means is that, while foods formulated for *all life stages of cats* are designed to meet normal nutritional needs of cats of all ages, some individuals, particularly older ones or those predisposed to certain health problems, may get far more of certain nutrients than they need.

Ingredients list: Ingredients are supposed to be listed in descending order of predominance by weight, but this can be somewhat misleading. For example, meat may be listed first, leading the consumer to believe the product contains mostly meat, when, in reality, the summation of separately listed grains and cereals makes plant material the predominant ingredient. Some labeling terms are strictly regulated, while others are not. For example, the title wording of "Chicken for Cats," "Chicken Platter," "Chicken Entree," and others,

can have different meanings in terms of the percentage of chicken the product must contain. A good way to check specific ingredient amounts is simply to call the manufacturer's toll-free number on the package and ask for the data. Many companies have consulting veterinarians and/or nutritionists, and you can judge for yourself how willing and able they seem to be to share information and answer your questions. A manufacturer's long-standing reputation can offer some assurance that correct product standards are met and maintained.

Dry weight analysis: Because label percentages are based on the entire food formula, water and all, one must standardize the base of comparison when reading labels of dry, canned, and semimoist foods in order to analyze and compare the ingredients. This is done

Most cat foods on the market today contain acidifying ingredients that help maintain better urinary tract health in cats of all ages.

by calculating the dry weight, the food content that would be left if all of the water were removed. First, determine the percentages of moisture and dry matter in the food. The guaranteed analysis already contains part of this information. If the label says the moisture content is 78 percent, subtract that figure from 100 percent (total food formula) to calculate the dry matter. In this case, the dry matter in the food is 22 percent.

Once you've calculated the dry matter, you can do a dry weight analysis for each nutrient in the food based on the label guarantees. The formula for this is simple:

$$\frac{\% \text{ Nutrient}}{\% \text{ Dry Matter}}$$

For example, we've already determined that the dry matter is 22 percent; now we want to know how much of that matter is protein. The guaranteed analysis on the label says the food contains a minimum of 10 percent crude protein. (The word *crude* simply means that the maximum or minimum amount was determined by laboratory assay.) That 10 percent figure is based on the food's total formula, including moisture content; however, on a dry matter basis, the protein content is:

$$\frac{0.10 \ (\% \text{ Protein})}{0.22 \ (\% \text{ Dry Matter})} = 0.45 = 45\%$$

To support normal growth and reproduction, AAFCO recommends that at least 30 percent of a cat's diet be protein. For maintenance of adult cats, protein content should be at least 26 percent. These are recommended minimum amounts, based on dry matter, that foods should contain. In this example, the label guarantees the product to be no less than 45 percent protein (dry weight basis), but it doesn't tell you whether the actual protein content exceeds that stated minimum. This information might be important if, for example, your cat requires a protein-reduced diet.

Although the dry weight analysis is a good way to compare nutrient percentages in different types of foods, it's not an exact measurement of daily nutrient intake. Remember, label guarantees are expressed either in minimum (not less than) or maximum (not more than) percentages, but not in actual amounts. If you're concerned about feeding too much or too little of a certain ingredient, consult your

This mother Ragdoll is a mitted chocolate lynx, a new colorpoint pattern that adds a striking striped effect.

veterinarian, who can best judge your Ragdoll's individual nutritional needs.

Feeding Guidelines

As a guide to daily rations, follow the feeding instructions on the package and measure out the recommended portions. Keep in mind that feeding guidelines are based on average nutritional needs and, therefore, are not intended to be used as absolute amounts. Some individuals may need greater portions, some less.

Most adult cats thrive on two meals a day, morning and evening. Others do well on a canned food breakfast, combined with ample dry food left out for free-choice nibbling. Whatever routine works best for you and your cat, your Ragdoll will feel more secure if you feed it at the same time and in the same place each day.

Homemade Diets

Because food is often viewed as a symbolic love offering, many people like to express their affection for their cats by preparing home-cooked meals and snacks for them. But constructing a complete and balanced meal for a cat from scratch is not as easy as it sounds—it is a chore best left to the experts. That's because cats are carnivores by nature, which means they must have protein from animal sources to stay healthy. They cannot safely adapt to a vegetarian diet, nor can they thrive solely on "people food." Their nutritional needs are significantly different from those of humans, dogs, and other mammals.

Reputable pet food manufacturers budget substantial amounts of money for research to back claims that their products provide "complete and balanced" nutrition for the various feline life stages. Without expert guidance, the home-based chef cannot guarantee an adequate mix of proteins, carbohydrates, fats, vitamins, minerals, and amino acids essential for maintaining good health in cats.

One amino acid in particular, *taurine*, is indispensable, because the cat cannot manufacture this essential ingredient on its own. Research has shown that if a cat's food is taurine-deficient, the animal stands a greater risk of developing blindness or a heart muscle disease called *dilated cardiomyopathy*. Prompted by such findings, manufacturers began routinely adding taurine to their commercial cat food products in the late 1980s, and since then, reported cases of dilated cardiomyopathy have declined dramatically.

Because the feline diet requires a delicate balance of numerous ingredients to maintain proper body functions and cell growth, too much or too little can be harmful. For this reason, home-cooked diets should be fed only in rare situations, such as when a cat is suspected of being allergic to an ingredient common in commercially prepared foods. Even then, the makeup of any routine homemade feline diet requires close supervision by a veterinarian with some expertise in animal nutrition.

This does not mean, however, that your cat is barred from ever sampling your home cooking or from tasting any tidbits of people food. On the contrary, such treats are okay on occasion, as long as you don't overdo it. Just keep the portions small, and don't make such offerings a daily habit, or your cat may begin turning up its nose at its own food. Remember, table scraps and people foods do not provide a complete and balanced diet for cats.

Also, garbage is garbage, so *never* feed your Ragdoll scraps that you would not eat. Also, do not feed bones, as these may splinter and lodge in your cat's throat or puncture parts of the digestive tract, leading to life-threatening complications.

Obesity

Obesity is a major health concern. If you're not careful, offering too many treats or too much *people food* can result in a fat cat. Obesity is probably the most common nutritional disorder among pets in the United States today. Moderately active or sedate cats that live in apartments and have little opportunity to exercise seem especially prone to developing this health disorder. But any cat, regardless of breed, can become fat if consistently overfed.

As in humans, obesity in cats can pose some serious health risks. The extra weight puts a strain on all organ systems and contributes to a shortened life span—and an overweight cat is a greater surgical and anesthetic risk.

The best way to judge whether a cat is overweight or underweight is to visually assess its body condition. This is not as easy as it sounds, however, because *ideal* weight varies from one individual to another, depending on a cat's age, sex, and other factors. In general, a cat is too fat if you cannot feel its ribs without having to probe with your fingers through thick, fleshy layers. Fat cats also often have sagging, pendulous bellies, bulges around the neck, and heavy accumulations of fat at the base of the tail. If you're unsure whether your cat is at ideal weight, simply ask your veterinarian during your cat's annual checkup.

Cats become fat for the same reasons that humans do—too many calories and too little exercise. While many cats with free access to food self-regulate their consumption appropriately, others overeat out of boredom. For this reason, when feeding dry food free-choice, it is best to measure and leave out only the recommended amount per day or per meal, depending on your feeding routine. Check the product's feeding guidelines for recommended amounts, and adjust the portions as needed to help your cat maintain its ideal body condition. Owners often unwittingly contribute to the problem of overeating by leaving out huge amounts of dry food that could last for days.

Snacks: Many owners enhance their cats' waistlines by offering too many high-fat, high-calorie gourmet snacks between meals. This situation is quite common, because so many people associate love and affection with offering food. While there's nothing wrong with offering your Ragdoll an occasional treat, remember not to overdo it. Also, don't substitute foods intended as treats for your cat's regular daily rations. Many commercial cat treats sold in stores are not labeled as *complete and balanced*. That's because they don't have to be, when they are intended only for intermittent use, and not for daily rations.

Feeding cats together: Some overweight cases may result from feeding cats together, which encourages competition. In addition, many cats tend to gain weight as they grow older, simply because they play less and need fewer calories.

Medical conditions: Weight gain and weight loss also can be symptoms of serious underlying medical conditions, such as diabetes, thyroid disorders, and kidney disease. Therefore, a veterinary examination is in order

Seal point Ragdoll.

Blue point mitted Ragdoll.

Blue cream point.

Choose a high-quality commercial cat food that is labeled as "complete and balanced" for your cat's current life stage.

before you reduce your cat's feed or attempt to put it on any special diet.

Therapeutic Diets

Your veterinarian can recommend an appropriate weight-loss method to suit your cat's particular situation. Some veterinarians prefer to use a good weight-reduction therapeutic diet, while others recommend continuing on the usual food, but cutting back the amount fed and eliminating all treats.

Therapeutic weight-reduction diets are nutritionally balanced but lower in calories to produce weight loss without creating other deficiencies. They are also higher in fiber to promote a feeling of fullness in the animal. If your veterinarian recommends a therapeutic diet, and you have more than one cat, you may have to feed the one on the special diet separately.

Whatever method is used to achieve feline weight loss, owner compliance is the key to its success. It's also important that any weight loss be gradual and that changes in diet or food portions also be accomplished gradually, over a one- to two-week period. Putting an overweight cat on a crash or starvation diet can result in a serious, potentially life-threatening liver disorder, called *hepatic lipidosis*.

KEEPING YOUR RAGDOLL CAT HEALTHY

Preventive Health Care

Keeping your Ragdoll indoors is the least expensive preventive health care measure you can provide your new companion. An indoor cat is less likely to contract an illness from a free-roaming animal or to fall victim to other outdoor hazards.

Getting annual veterinary checkups for your Ragdoll and adhering to a routine vaccination schedule are two more ways to benefit both your cat and your pocketbook. Your Ragdoll will have a better opportunity to enjoy a longer, healthier life, and you can save money by preventing problems instead of treating them. The cost of aggressively treating a single serious illness can quickly surpass the money you spend on yearly physicals and routine booster shots throughout your Ragdoll's lifetime.

Choosing a Veterinarian

Try to find a veterinarian who has had previous experience in treating Ragdoll cats or, at least, is familiar with the breed. Because Ragdolls are relatively rare compared to some other breeds, some veterinarians have treated few or none of them. So, if your breeder is local, ask for a recommendation. Then, schedule a post-purchase veterinary exam within one or two weeks after you bring your new cat home.

During your Ragdoll's first visit to the veterinarian, discuss the need for any blood work or other tests to determine the status of your new cat's health. For example, you should request a stool analysis to rule out the presence of internal parasites (see the chart on page 54). An infected queen can pass certain worms to her kittens through the placenta and through the breast milk. If the examination reveals parasites, your veterinarian will recommend appropriate treatment. Because deworming agents can cause toxic reactions, these drugs should be administered only under veterinary supervision. An effective parasite prevention program includes keeping cats indoors, maintaining good sanitation, and controlling fleas, rodents, and other vermin.

Signs of Illness

With proper nutrition, regular veterinary checkups, good dental care, and routine vaccinations, you can reasonably expect your Ragdoll to live an average of 10 to 15 years. When

Blue point Ragdoll.

Internal Parasites

	Symptoms	Mode of Transmission
Tapeworms Appropriate flea-control measures are preventive	Fresh segments passed in stool look like white, wriggling grains of rice	Rodents and fleas; cats ingest fleas during self-grooming; larvae mature inside cat's intestines
Roundworms	Vomiting; diarrhea; weight loss; potbelly; overall poor condition; white, spaghetti-like strands may be visible in vomit or stool	Contact with contaminated cat feces; kittens may contract from infected mothers
Hookworms	Anemia; diarrhea; weight loss; black, tarry stools	Larvae-infested soil; more prevalent in hot, humid areas
Heartworms Preventive medication recommended in high-risk regions	Shortness of breath, coughing, periodic vomiting	Mosquito bites; more prevalent in humid, mosquito-plagued regions
Lungworms	Dry, persistent cough	Contact with infected cats; eating infected birds or rodents

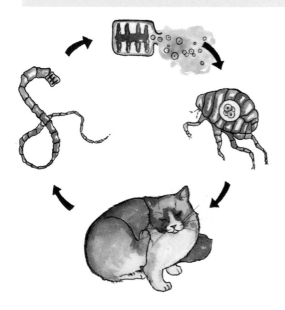

illness does strike, however, you as the owner, must be prepared to recognize the signs and symptoms and seek veterinary care right away. By recognizing a problem early and seeking treatment, you can greatly improve your cat's chances of a full recovery.

Changes in appetite: Often, the first telltale sign that something is wrong is a sudden change in appetite. That's why any marked change in normal eating habits should be regarded with suspicion and carefully watched. If the problem

Fleas can carry tapeworm larvae, which your Ragdoll may ingest as it grooms itself. The larvae grow into long, segmented strands within a cat's intestines.

External Parasites

	Symptoms	Mode of Transmission
Fleas: even indoor cats are commonly plagued by these tiny, biting insects that feed on blood	Excessive scratching, presence of *flea dirt* (tiny black specks of flea excrement that turn bloody when dampened) in fur	Effective one-spot, once-a-month flea control medications are available through veterinarians
Ticks: some ticks carry Lyme disease, which humans can catch	Felt as a bump in the cat's fur after tick burrows head into skin and swells from sucking blood	Remove tick promptly by grasping and pulling straight out with tweezers (wear rubber gloves)
Lice: uncommon in well-kept, healthy cats	White specks (nits) stuck to fur	Clip coat and bathe cat with medicated shampoo available through veterinarians
Mites: most common variety found in the cat is the *ear mite*, which borrows in the ear canal and can cause serious inner ear infection	Itchiness; hair loss; crusty sores; scaly dandruff; body odor; *ear mites:* crumbly, waxy, brown buildup in ears; head shaking; scratching at ears; holding ears to side of head	Veterinarian must identify specific mite variety before dispensing appropriate medication; other cats and dogs in household may require treatment also, due to contagion
Ringworm: not a worm at all but a fungus; prompt treatment is required, as infection can spread from cats to humans	Itchiness; scaly skin; patchy hair loss	Clip coat, bathe cat, disinfect pet bedding, administer medications as recommended by a veterinarian; a noncore vaccine is preventive in high-risk households where ringworm has been a past problem

doesn't resolve itself quickly—within 24 hours or so—report your observations to your veterinarian.

Changes in litter box habits: Sudden changes in toilet habits should be investigated for medical causes. If you notice that your Ragdoll is missing the litter box, straining to urinate, urinating more often, passing bloody urine, or urinating in unusual places, suspect a lower urinary tract infection or blockage and seek medical attention right away (see page 50).

Other trouble signs include unexplained or rapid weight loss, increased thirst, frequent vomiting or diarrhea, coughing, sneezing, bleeding, staggering, swellings, panting, lethargy, lameness, coat changes, nasal discharge, bloody stool, crouching in a hunched-up position, hiding in

unusual places, and difficulty breathing. The list is by no means complete. Because cats can succumb rapidly to illness, don't delay in seeking veterinary help at the first hint of trouble.

Vaccination

Several infectious diseases common in cats are caused by airborne organisms that can waft into your home on a breeze through open doors and windows. Even your hands, shoes, and clothing can serve as transmission modes, silently tracking in deadly disease-causing organisms. Fortunately, highly effective vaccines exist to combat many feline diseases, and that's why it's important to keep recommended vaccinations current, even if your Ragdoll stays inside all the time.

A healthy bicolor Ragdoll.

Booster Shots

Traditionally, veterinarians have given yearly booster shots to maintain adequate immunity. But recent studies suggest that immunity with certain vaccines may last much longer than once thought. This new knowledge, combined with heightened concerns about soft-tissue tumors occurring at common vaccination sites (see page 59), prompted some practitioners to revisit their views on vaccine protocol.

Vaccination Schedule

Core vaccines protect against severe or easily transmitted diseases and are recommended for *all* cats. The core diseases include *rabies, feline distemper,* and two upper respiratory illnesses, *rhinotracheitis* and *calicivirus.* According to the new guidelines, most cats should get core vaccine boosters once every three years. However, cats with a greater risk of exposure may still need booster shots once a year, or as recommended by your veterinarian.

Noncore vaccines are recommended for cats at highest risk of exposure to *feline leukemia virus (FeLV), feline infectious peritonitis (FIP), chlamydia (feline pneumonitis),* and *ringworm.* These vaccines are considered optional and should be administered based on the risk of exposure. In addition, yearly boostering for cats receiving this protection is still recommended.

Kittens acquire a degree of immunity to disease from their mother's first milk, called the "colostrum," but this protection wanes in a short time.

Establishing Initial Immunity

Most experts still agree that the *ideal* vaccination schedule begins with giving kittens their first combination core shot for upper respiratory infections and feline distemper at approximately 6 to 8 weeks of age. Between 8 and 12 weeks of age, the first in a series of two shots for feline leukemia virus (FeLV) may be given. At 12 weeks of age, another shot for upper respiratory infections and distemper is administered. Then, between 12 and 16 weeks, kittens get a rabies shot, plus the second shot in the FeLV series. A year later, all vaccinations should be repeated and thereafter followed up with periodic boosters on a schedule recommended by your veterinarian.

Vaccine Reactions

Although side effects from vaccines are minimal in most cases, breeders say that some Ragdolls do seem to be more sensitive to

Feline Diseases

	Symptoms	Prognosis
Feline Viral Rhinotracheitis (FVR) Highly contagious respiratory ailment caused by herpes virus; core vaccine is preventive	Sneezing; nasal discharge; crusty, watering eyes; appetite loss; lethargy	High mortality rate; survivors may become chronic carriers and shed virus during stress
Feline Calicivirus (FCV) Serious upper respiratory infection; core vaccine is preventive	Similar to FVR, with painful tongue, mouth ulcers, sore muscles, stiff gait, limping	May progress to pneumonia; survivors may become carriers
Feline Panleukopenia Virus (FPV) Also called *feline distemper, feline parvovirus* (unrelated to canine parvovirus), or *feline infectious enteritis*; core vaccine is preventive	Appetite loss, fever, depression, vomiting yellow bile, painful abdomen, low white cell count (leukopenia)	Often fatal, highly contagious among cats
Feline Chlamydiosis Respiratory infection, also called *feline pneumonitis*; noncore vaccine	Similar to FVR and FCV, with weepy eyes, swollen eyelids	Quite contagious, especially among kittens
Rabies Core vaccine is preventive and required by law in many localities	Personality changes; irritability; paralysis to facial, throat muscles; drooling saliva	Fatal; transmissible to humans and other mammals from infected animal's saliva via bite, open wound, or scrape
Feline Leukemia Virus (FeLV) Noncore vaccine is preventive; testing recommended to determine positive or negative status	Weight loss, anemia, poor appetite, lethargy, recurring infections	Often fatal, but infected cats may survive several years; impaired immune system may lead to cancers, secondary ailments
Feline Infectious Peritonitis (FIP) If exposure risk is high, noncore "nose drop" vaccine recommended	Fever, lethargy, appetite and weight loss, labored breathing, swollen belly	Potentially fatal; may affect internal organs; hazard in multicat households
Feline Immunodeficiency Virus (FIV), *cannot* be transmitted to humans; keeping cats indoors is preventive	Lethargy, weight loss, gum disease, chronic infections, weakened immune system	No current cure or vaccine; virus spreads among cats through bites
Feline Lower Urinary Tract Disease	See page 50; also "Changes in litter box habits," page 55	

certain shots than others, particularly the FeLV and rabies vaccines.

In addition, recent research has raised concerns about a low incidence of tumors, called *fibrosarcomas*, developing at the injection sites of FeLV and rabies vaccines. While not caused by the vaccines directly, the tumors appear to result from a profound localized inflammation some cats experience, perhaps in reaction to the aluminum compounds used in the vaccine suspension.

As the matter remains under investigation, more veterinarians are recommending FeLV vaccination *only* for cats at greatest risk of contracting the disease, which is why the vaccine is considered noncore, or optional. Cats allowed outdoors or frequently exposed to other cats have the highest risk of FeLV exposure and certainly should be vaccinated.

Regardless of breed, it is fairly common for some cats to experience mild lethargy for a day or two after receiving their shots. But some vaccine reactions can be serious, causing convulsions, labored breathing, and even death. It is important to talk to your veterinarian about which vaccines your Ragdoll may not readily tolerate.

Allergic Conditions

Cats can develop allergies to pollen, weeds, grasses, mold spores, house dust, feathers, wool, insect stings, drugs, chemicals, and food ingredients. Cats' symptoms involve itchy skin, face, and ears. Typical warning signs include compulsive rubbing against furniture or carpet and excessive scratching, licking, or chewing at itchy places. Gastrointestinal symptoms such as vomiting and diarrhea also can occur, particu-

larly if the allergen, or allergy-causing substance, is ingested in a food or drug. Redness, crusty skin, and hair loss around the nose, mouth, and face suggest a food allergy, or possibly an allergy to plastic feeding dishes. In the latter case, replacing plastic dishes with lead-free ceramic or stainless steel dishes offers an easy remedy.

Most allergy cases are not so simple. Testing exists, but allergies remain difficult to diagnose. Treatment varies widely from patient to patient. Recovery can take a long time, and owners may have to reduce the allergen in the cat's environment for as long as the animal lives.

Flea Allergy Dermatitis

The most common allergy condition seen in the cat is caused by fleas, and even indoor cats are not immune. Fleas lay eggs on the host and turn your Ragdoll's plush, dense fur into a virtual nursery for millions more. As the cat moves and scratches, the eggs fall off into your carpets, upholstery, and bedding, where they hatch and begin the cycle anew.

The unsightly skin condition that results, called *flea allergy dermatitis*, is characterized by itchiness, hair loss, patchy redness (called "hot spots"), and scabby, crusty sores on the skin. Appropriate medications dispensed by your veterinarian to relieve symptoms and diligent flea control measures help lessen the condition's severity and occurrence.

Effective flea control used to require an expensive arsenal of products designed to treat the pet and its environment at various phases of the flea's complex life cycle. This arsenal included sprays, dips, powders, flea collars, medicated shampoos, and room foggers, all

Dental care is important for cats, too. Your veterinarian will check your cat's teeth at each annual visit.

elastic or breakaway sections to make them safer. The recent introduction of one-spot, once-a-month flea control products for cats has made effective flea control much easier. Ask your veterinarian about them.

Dental Care

Cats are not prone to getting cavities, but they are susceptible to gum disease, which can eventually lead to tooth loss. Dental disease can also silently compromise your cat's immune system and overall health by allowing bacteria to leak into the bloodstream from pockets of pus around sore, infected gums. Normal, healthy gums are pink, but diseased gums are tender, red and swollen—signs of *gingivitis* (inflamed gums) caused by plaque and tartar buildup.

Left untreated, this condition causes the gums to recede gradually and the teeth to loosen. Bad breath is a cardinal sign of dental disease. A cat with dental problems may also have difficulty eating because its teeth and gums hurt, and as a result, may lose weight and condition.

targeted to kill or control fleas at the egg, larval, pupal, or adult stages. Often, these products failed to be effective when applied during the wrong life cycle of the insect and required repeating. They could also be potentially dangerous if used inappropriately or in combination with incompatible products. Even flea collars, although easy to use, posed a risk of strangling or choking, unless designed with

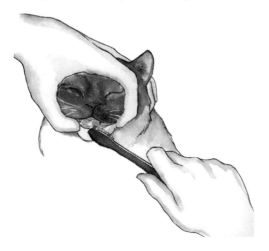

To brush your Ragdoll's teeth, grasp the head from above with one hand, using the fingers to hold open the corners of the lips. With the other hand, gently brush the outside surfaces of the teeth with a soft toothbrush or with your finger wrapped in gauze. Cleaning the inside surfaces of the teeth is usually not necessary.

The best way to prevent such problems is to regularly brush or rinse your cat's teeth with oral hygiene products designed for use in animals. Your veterinarian can recommend an appropriate mouth rinse or a nonfoaming, enzymatic toothpaste made especially for animals and demonstrate the proper use of these products. From time to time, you may need to have your Ragdoll's teeth professionally cleaned. For this procedure, the cat is anesthetized, and the veterinarian uses an ultrasonic scaler to blast away the ugly, brown tartar and polish the teeth.

Medicating Your Ragdoll

Getting your Ragdoll used to having its mouth opened and handled will make it much easier for you to give it oral medications, should the need arise. Otherwise, the ordeal is likely to be a two-person job, with one person holding the cat while the other administers the medicine. Pills and liquids are the most common forms of medication you will likely have to administer. But whether your cat's condition calls for oral medications, injections, eye ointments, ear drops, or force-feeding that you must do at home, ask your veterinarian to explain and demonstrate the best method of application. Make sure you understand how and when to administer any medication before you attempt to do it yourself, and know what to expect in terms of recovery time and side effects.

Never give your Ragdoll any drug or over-the-counter drugs or remedies meant for humans. Tylenol and similar products that contain an ingredient called *acetaminophen*, are especially deadly to cats, even in small amounts. Aspirin products can also be lethal to cats.

Preventing Hair Balls

Hair balls are soft, tubular masses of ingested hair. Cats can swallow a lot of loose hair as they groom themselves, particularly at the height of shedding season. Normally, this creates no problem; the hair simply moves through the digestive tract and gets eliminated in the usual way. Occasionally, however, too much hair accumulates in the stomach and is vomited back up as a hair ball. In more serious cases, the hair may form a large mass further along in the digestive tract, causing a blockage and requiring an enema or even surgery to remove. Signs of a blockage include refusal to eat or regurgitating food shortly after eating.

Regular grooming is the easiest and cheapest way to prevent hair balls. Brushing and combing your Ragdoll helps remove the loose, dead hair it would otherwise swallow.

If your cat makes a habit of spitting up hair balls on your carpets, several petrolatum-based hair ball pastes are available through veterinarians or at pet supply stores. These products help lubricate the hair mass so that the cat expels it more easily. Grass also seems to act as a purgative to help cats expel excess hair from the stomach. You can grow a fresh supply of grass indoors for your cat, and most pet stores sell *kitty grass* kits specifically for this purpose. Most cats love to nibble on greenery, and providing your Ragdoll with its own personal supply of grass may help keep it from grazing on your house plants.

UNDERSTANDING YOUR RAGDOLL CAT

Interpreting "Feline-Speak"

Ragdolls have an extensive vocabulary of mews and meows, as do all cats, however, they are quiet, soft-spoken cats that seldom resort to "talking" unless doing so is absolutely necessary to make themselves understood.

Vocal Sounds

According to the intonation, a cat's meow can express many moods and needs. For example, a loud, throaty howl, or an urgent yowl, demands attention; it may mean that your cat is in distress—or that it simply wants something to eat. Queens in heat belt out a particularly annoying mating call to the neighborhood toms that's loud and persistent enough to rattle the senses. Mother cats, on the other hand, chirp softly, in a most comforting and soothing way, when calling to their kittens.

Purring

The most universally recognized and beloved feline sound of all, the purr, is also the most mysterious. Experts still puzzle over the exact mechanism that causes or enables big cats and domestic cats alike to purr. Most scientists say the sound is probably produced by vibrations in

Blue cream point.

the larynx, or voice box, as the cat breathes in and out. By whatever means, your Ragdoll can control and produce this most soothing feline sound of all at will.

But *why* cats purr is really more mysterious than *how* they do it. Even kittens as young as two days old can purr, suggesting that the sound may be a special form of bonding between mother and offspring, the purpose of which may be to communicate and reassure that all is well in the nest. This theory seems plausible, given the fact that, for human caretakers, cuddling a purring cat can help relieve stress, promote a mutual sense of well-being, and strengthen the human/feline bond. Perhaps by purring in the presence of a caretaker, cats are responding as they would to a "parent cat," communicating that everything is okay.

Of course, there is a long-held belief that cats purr to express contentment, when they feel happy, secure, warm, and well fed. But they've also been known to purr when nervous (at the veterinarian's office), upset, sick, hurt, or hungry. Interestingly, cats have even been observed purring as they succumb to the final grip of death. As a result, the generally accepted theory is that cats purr not only to express pleasure, but also to calm and comfort themselves when faced with an unpleasant situation.

Body Language

Feline-ese involves more than just purring, mewing, and meowing. Cats let their elegant bodies do most of the talking, and they communicate eloquently with their feline and human companions alike. A particular body stance, a simple turn of the tail, or the flick of an ear all can have specific meaning. For example, when your Ragdoll walks toward you with ears pricked forward and tail held high, with just the tip slightly bending forward, he or she is saying, "Hello, my friend. It's sure good to see ya!"

When confronted by a stranger or an adversary, however, a timid or submissive cat crouches, lowers its ears and drops its tail. A frightened or defensive cat can make itself appear as large as possible by arching its back and fully fluffing out its fur. An angry cat also crouches low, but its stance and tail action differs from that of the submissive cat. With ears flattened, muscles tense and ready to spring to action, the angry cat appears poised to attack. The flicking of its tail from side to side clearly signals a warning, "Back off!" If that posture fails to get the message across, a loud hiss or a low, drawn-out growl leaves no doubt that an attack is imminent.

The Primary Senses

Much of the mystery associated with felines is a direct result of their unique anatomy, which endows them with their special night-time hunting prowess. The cat's mastery of the night has sparked awe, envy, and fear in the human soul throughout the ages—enough, at various times in history, to elevate this superbly adapted nocturnal hunter to the status of a god or damn the entire species as devils.

A cat possesses five known senses, which are far superior to ours. Understanding how your Ragdoll perceives its world through these highly developed senses helps explain many feline behaviors that appear incomprehensible otherwise.

Sense of Sight

As primarily nocturnal hunters, cats possess excellent night vision. Although they have poor color vision, cats can see much better in dim light than humans can, but they cannot see in total darkness. There must be some minimal light available for the feline eye to amplify. This ability stems from a special layer of cells behind the feline retina, called the *tapetum lucidum,* which makes a cat's eyes appear to glow in the dark. These specialized cells act like a mirror, reflecting all available light back onto the retina and giving the cat its exceptional ability to see well in low-light conditions.

The feline pupil can also dilate much wider than the human eye. This allows the cat's eye to collect light more effectively in dim conditions. A cat that feels threatened, frightened, or defensive will dilate its pupils to see better over a wider area. Of course, the cat's pupil works the other way, too. On sunny days, the pupils constrict to vertical slits to block out bright light.

Well suited to hunting and night-stalking, a cat's eyes are especially adept at detecting the slightest movements made by small prey animals. Many prey animals have evolved with the instinct to freeze in place and remain perfectly still when they detect the scent or presence of a nearby predator. A stalking cat hard at work will crouch patiently for long periods, staring at nothing, or so it appears, until the concealed

A cat's eyes appear to glow in the dark because a special layer of cells in the eye, called the **tapetum lucidum***, acts like a mirror, reflecting available light back onto the retina. This gives the cat its exceptional night vision.*

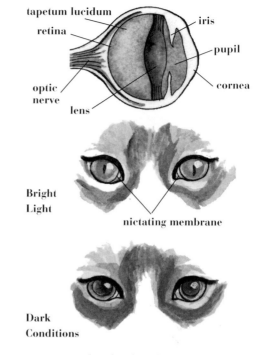

or camouflaged prey finally reveals its where-abouts with barely a twitch in the grass.

Another special characteristic of the cat's eye is an opaque third eyelid, called the *nictitating membrane*, which helps protect and lubricate the eyeball. Although usually not visible under normal conditions (except occasionally when the cat is sleeping), the third eyelid may protrude from the eye's inside corner if the eye gets injured, irritated, or infected. In addition, this white, filmy membrane is sometimes more visible over the eyes with certain diseases and, therefore, warrants a veterinary examination if it persists beyond an occasional, sleepy blink.

Sense of Smell

Cats possess an acute sense of smell, far superior to that of humans, but definitely not as good as that of dogs. As with dogs and other animals, cats use odors and the sense of smell to identify each other as well as objects in their territory. For example, when two cats meet on friendly terms, they typically engage in a ritual of sniffing each other about the head and anal areas, where scent glands exude a vast databank of personal information. Among cats, this behavior is the equivalent of the human handshake and hello.

Jacobson's organ: As part of their sense of smell, cats and many other mammals have a special scent mechanism, called the

vomeronasal or *Jacobson's organ*. This specialized scent organ adds a different dimension to animals' ability to detect and identify odors and is believed to give mammals an edge on finding mates by helping them sort out sex-related scent hormones called *pheromones*.

Located in the roof of the mouth behind the incisor teeth, this special organ actually allows cats to taste odor molecules. When using the Jacobson's organ, a cat curls its upper lip back and, with teeth bared and mouth partially agape, sniffs the air deeply through both nose and mouth. This grimace, often mistaken for a silent growl or a snarl, is called the *flehmen* response. Like many animals, cats sometimes display flehmen when examining urine and scent marks left by other animals and during territorial or mating rituals.

Sense of Taste

Specialized cells on your Ragdoll's tongue enable it to detect the chemical components of food as saliva dissolves them in the mouth. These taste buds send signals along nerve pathways to the brain, where taste identification actually takes place. The food with the greatest appeal to a carnivore's palate is, of course, meat. And being naturally evolved meat-eating predators, cats like their meals lukewarm, preferably as near the body temperature of most small prey mammals as possible—not hot, and certainly not cold, as in straight out of the refrigerator.

Pet food industry taste preference tests suggest that cats can distinguish between salty or sour foods, but they cannot taste simple sug-

Seal bicolor Ragdoll: In feline body language, a cat is being friendly when it walks toward you with tail held high and ears pricked forward.

ars. According to the experts, this means that cats generally should not prefer sweet or sugary foods, although we've all heard owners' tales about cats that would kill for a chocolate chip cookie. But since many sweets are also high in fat, the cat with the sweet tooth is probably craving the yummy taste of the high fat ingredients, and not the sugar.

Sense of Touch

Your Ragdoll's whiskers are highly sensitive tactile organs, so *never* clip them. There's a common saying that if a cat's whiskers can pass through a small opening, the cat knows the rest of its body can fit through and follow. This may be more fancy than fact (especially since obesity is such a common problem among today's house cats); however, cats do use their whiskers to sense and avoid objects in dim light and to detect vibrations and changes in their environment. Cats also use their whiskers to touch and gauge the size of prey caught in their paws.

Sense of Hearing

Few people are surprised to learn that cats can hear better than humans. Because their normal prey typically emits high-pitched sounds, cats' ears are tuned to frequencies well beyond the range of human hearing. Cats can also quickly learn to recognize the source and meaning of certain sounds; for example, chirping

Unless you intend to become a professional breeder, have your Ragdoll spayed or neutered.

birds mean a possible meal is nearby. This associative ability extends from the hunting ground into the household, and after the first time or two, your Ragdoll will come running to the buzz of an electric can opener, the whisk of a pop-top lid, or the opening of the refrigerator door. And if you consistently call your Ragdoll by name at each feeding, it will quickly learn its name, and perhaps even come when called.

An Added Sense of Balance

Besides their five primary senses, cats also possess an extraordinary sense of balance. If a cat rolls off a windowsill and falls in an upside-down position, a balance mechanism in the inner ear enables the cat to rotate its forequarters first, then the hindquarters, so that it automatically rights itself in midair and lands on all fours. This remarkable ability is known as the *righting reflex*. The cat's supple and flexible spine also contributes to its maneuverability in free-fall. Even with these impressive assets, however, cats that fall from great heights can

Cats often sleep about 18 hours a day.

neutering tend to curb this undesirable behavior. But both sexes, whether whole or altered, may occasionally resort to spraying when engaged in a dispute with another cat over territory or dominance.

Clawing

When a cat scratches the arm of the couch, it is not misbehaving. Like spraying and rubbing, this action, too, is an instinctive territorial marking behavior. The cat is actually marking the scratched object with scent from glands in its paws. The cat is also fulfilling an instinctive need to keep its basic defense weaponry—its claws—sharp and trim. Similar to filing fingernails, the in-and-out action on wood, carpet, or rough fabric helps strip away the dead, outer layers of the claws.

Outdoor cats can often be observed marking and sharpening their claws on the trunks of trees. For an indoor cat, this perfectly natural feline behavior can become a problem when the scent that's left behind on your furniture, combined with an apparent preference for the spot, continues to draw the cat back to the same site to claw until the couch arm becomes a shredded mess.

You cannot eliminate the cat's instinctive need to claw, but you can modify and redirect the behavior by providing your Ragdoll with a suitable scratching post. Inappropriate clawing habits, once firmly established, can be difficult to break, so begin teaching your Ragdoll kitten to use a scratching post early, as soon as you bring it home (see page 26).

You cannot eliminate the cat's instinctive need to claw, but you can modify the behavior by providing your Ragdoll with a carpeted cat tree.

Destructive Clawing

Vinyl Nail Caps

Once a destructive clawing habit becomes firmly entrenched, one humane alternative for dealing with the problem is to glue vinyl nail caps onto a cat's freshly trimmed claws. These caps, which can be purchased through veterinarians, give the nails a soft, blunt tip and help prevent snags in carpets, furniture, and drapes. The major drawback to this method is that the vinyl caps have to be reapplied every four to six weeks, as the nails grow. The application is simple, however, and owners can purchase take-home kits and learn to manicure their cats' nails themselves. Ask your veterinarian to demonstrate the product. Vinyl nail caps are not recommended for outdoor animals because they inhibit a cat's ability to climb.

Declawing

This surgical procedure is the least desirable alternative for dealing with destructive clawing and should be considered only as a last resort after other methods have failed. Banned in some countries, this controversial procedure is still performed in the United States by veterinarians who consider it a viable option over having to euthanize the cat or surrender it to an animal shelter for adoption.

The declawing procedure involves putting the cat under anesthesia and surgically amputating the claw tip and the last bone of the toe. Generally, only the front claws are removed, because the hind feet are not used for scratching furniture. While this procedure may offer a permanent solution to destructive clawing problems, it is not painless. After the operation, the cat suffers some pain and risk of infection as its mutilated paws heal.

There are other drawbacks, too. Declawing renders a cat ineligible for the show ring, because the major cat associations that sponsor shows disallow the practice. With only the front claws removed, a cat still can use its rear claws to climb trees, but it just can't climb as well as before. The procedure clearly inhibits climbing and self-defense, which means that cats allowed to roam freely outdoors should not be declawed and disadvantaged in this way.

Many people believe that robbing a cat of its natural defenses with this procedure may harm the animal psychologically and make it more apt to bite in self-defense. Some owners report profound personality changes in their cats after the surgery. Others say their cats developed inappropriate toilet habits afterward, probably as a result of cat box litter irritating the tender incisions. Older cats seem to have more difficulty adjusting to life without claws than kittens.

Handling House-Soiling

Destructive clawing and house-soiling are the major behavior problems that often land many cats in animal shelters. Some owners either don't understand the motivating factors well enough to deal with them, or they simply give up too soon and give away the cat.

Often, what people perceive as a behavior *problem* in the home is quite normal for cats

living in the wild. Understanding what is normal behavior for cats under natural conditions is crucial to understanding how to deal with them when things go wrong under confined conditions. Knowing what motivates a certain behavior is the key to figuring out how to modify or correct it.

If you have more than one cat, you can help prevent elimination problems by providing each animal with its own litter box. Even then, the more aggressive cat may sometimes chase another away from the litter box. If this happens, place the boxes far enough apart, in separate rooms or at opposite ends of the house, to give each cat a sense of privacy and individual territory.

Generally, when a housebroken cat eliminates outside its litter box, it is either marking territory or displaying a preference for a particular spot, surface, or litter box filler. Contrary to popular belief, cats do not begin house-soiling out of spite. At least, that's what the behavior experts say, although many owners can reel off accounts of cats urinating on shoes or other belongings of people who have irritated or neglected them. But such accounts are largely a matter of interpretation.

Whatever the cause, house-soiling is often symptomatic of emotional anxiety or physical discomfort. So whenever a cat begins eliminating in inappropriate places, consider urinary tract infections and other medical causes first (see pages 50 and 55 and chart on page 58) and take your Ragdoll to the veterinarian for a checkup. If the cause turns out to be physical, prompt medical

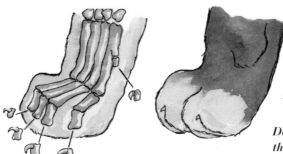

Declawing involves surgical amputation of the claw tips and the last bone of the toes.

treatment can reverse the problem before it becomes an established habit. Always rule out disease or infection first, then pursue the behavioral or emotional approaches.

Spraying vs. Urinating

If the urine stain appears to start primarily on a vertical surface—a wall or furniture leg—and drip down, then, the cat is *spraying* to mark territory. If the urine is pooled on a flat, horizontal surface—the floor or the bedcovers—then the cat is squatting to eliminate urine. Ascertaining this difference is crucial because the factors that motivate each type of behavior are different. To effectively deal with either undesirable behavior, you must try to eliminate the factors that appear to be causing or influencing the situation.

There are some common motivating factors behind house-soiling problems:

Location preference: A cat that squats and inappropriately urinates on the carpet or floor may simply be expressing a dislike for the location of its litter box or for the texture of the litter. Try moving the box to a quieter, more secluded part of the house, or if possible, place it at or near the site of the house-soiling "accident."

Litter preference: If location doesn't seem to be a motivating factor, experiment with different types and textures of kitty litter. Some cats don't like litters treated with fancy perfumes and deodorizers and will refuse to use them. Some cats prefer fine-grained litter that is like sand, while others are content with the larger, coarser clay granules.

Cleanliness: In many cases, failure to use the litter box occurs because cat and owner have different opinions as to what constitutes a clean litter box. The owner may think cleaning the box once a week is enough, but the cat may want it cleaned every day. Cats are fastidious creatures, and digging in dirty, damp litter must be disgusting to them. If you're equally fastidious about removing the solid waste daily and replacing soiled litter weekly, your cat likely will be more happily inclined to continue using the box without mishap.

Anxiety: Emotional causes of house-soiling are the most difficult to pinpoint. Sometimes the sight of outdoor cats or the introduction of a new pet or a new baby into the household can trigger territorial spraying. In this situation, veterinarians can prescribe drugs that may ease the cat's anxiety and help suppress spraying and aggressive behaviors.

Cleaning Up Accidents

When cleaning up carpet stains, remember to clean the mat under the carpet, too, as the urine will have soaked through. Any traces of scent left will continue to attract the cat back to the same spot. Several good odor-neutralizing products can be purchased at pet supply stores for cleaning up pet messes. A mix of white vinegar and warm water also works fairly well, but avoid ammonia-based cleaners. Ammonia is a urine by-product and might attract the cat back to the spot.

Make the surface less appealing to the cat by covering it temporarily with plastic, aluminum foil, sandpaper, window screen, or double-sided tape. If possible, keep the cat completely away from the area for awhile to break the habit. For a different approach, try changing the significance of the area by placing food and water bowls there. Cats typically will not eliminate where they eat.

GROOMING YOUR RAGDOLL CAT

Grooming Supplies

The Ragdoll's medium-length, mat-resistant, silky coat doesn't require quite the grooming commitment that some other longhaired breeds demand. Still, regular combing and brushing is essential to control shedding and to keep the coat looking nice.

Plus, with a longhaired cat in the house, you can reasonably expect to become intimately acquainted with your vacuum cleaner. While longhaired cats shed about the same amount as shorthaired cats, long hair is more noticeable on your furnishings, carpets, and clothes. Regular combing will help remove the loose cat hairs from your Ragdoll's coat before they have a chance to shed off onto your furniture. To easily wipe cat hair off your furnishings, keep a brush, lint remover, or a damp cloth handy.

To meet your cat's basic grooming needs, invest in nail clippers, several sizes of steel pet combs, and a natural bristle brush. For kittens, start grooming with small and medium-size steel combs, and save a wide-toothed one for use on adult cats. For flea control, purchase a fine-toothed comb. Once caught in the comb's closely-spaced teeth, fleas drown easily when dipped in a pan of water. A fine comb also readily removes flea dirt deep in the fur.

Blue bicolor Ragdoll.

Regular grooming is the best and least expensive way to prevent hair-ball problems in longhaired cats. Brushing also helps stimulate circulation and distribute natural oils through the coat, keeping the fur shiny and healthy looking. By grooming your Ragdoll on a regular basis—at least two or three times a week—you'll be much more likely to notice anything out of the ordinary, such as concealed cuts, scratches, lumps, or bumps that may warrant veterinary investigation, for example, or even a hidden tick that has latched on for a blood meal.

The general condition of the coat is a good indicator of overall health. For instance, you'll want to schedule a visit to the veterinarian if you ever notice that your Ragdoll's skin is looking dry or flaky, or if the coat appears dull, looks oily, smells bad, or feels brittle. Several medical and dietary problems can affect the skin and hair coat, including allergies, parasites, and hormonal or nutritional imbalances, among others.

Shedding

Most people assume that the seasonal changes of hair coat are caused by temperature changes, but that isn't entirely true. Experts say that environmental lighting primarily governs the shedding process in animals.

Regular grooming includes an inspection of the ears and eyes for discharge or debris.

Trim your cat's claws about once a month.

Cats retract their claws when not in use. To extend them for trimming, hold the paw with your thumb on top and fingers on the bottom and gently squeeze. Before clipping, look closely at the nail and identify the *quick*. If the nail is white, the quick clearly shows up as a thin pink line running about three-quarters of the way down the nail toward the tip. To avoid cutting into the sensitive quick, trim the nail tip below the pink line. The quick contains nerves and blood vessels, but the nail tip below it does not. If you accidentally cut too high up into the pink quick, the cat will feel pain and

Use a clean gauze pad or cotton ball to wipe the ear flaps clean.

Get your Ragdolls accustomed to grooming at an early age.

the nail will bleed. If this happens, hold pressure over the wound with a cotton ball until the blood clots, or apply a shaving styptic.

With the cat held securely in your lap or placed on the countertop or table where you do your routine grooming, trim the claws on the front and hind feet. Start by clipping just two or three nails at a time, then add more as your Ragdoll gets accustomed to the idea. Use human or pet nail clippers for the job, then smooth the rough edges with an emery board or nail file. Don't forget the fifth claw slightly higher up on each inside forepaw.

SHOWING YOUR RAGDOLL CAT

How Cat Shows Started

England is generally credited with staging the first cat show in 1871 at London's Crystal Palace. Harrison Weir organized the prototype of today's cat competitions and developed the first breed standards by which cats were judged in those days. Weir also was president of Great Britain's first cat club, the National Cat Club, which issued the first feline stud book in the late 1800s. By 1910, the Governing Council of the Cat Fancy (GCCF) was established with delegates from the various clubs to oversee the registering of pedigreed cats and to set the rules for all cat shows in Great Britain. The GCCF retains this function today.

In the United States, cat exhibits and judgings have taken place since the 1870s, but an official all-breed show held in 1895 at New York's Madison Square Garden marked the beginning of real interest among North American cat fanciers. In 1899, the first and oldest U.S. registry, the American Cat Association (ACA), was formed to keep records. Today, several other cat-registering associations exist in North America. They include the Cat Fanciers' Association (CFA), the American Cat Fanciers' Association (ACFA), the International Cat Asso-

The thrill of winning a rosette makes the hard work involved in showing cats worthwhile.

ciation (TICA), the Cat Fanciers' Federation (CFF), the American Association of Cat Enthusiasts (AACE), the National Cat Fanciers' Association (NCFA), the United Feline Organization (UFO), the Canadian Cat Association (CCA), and the Traditional Cat Association (TCA). Each association has its own show rules and breed standards, but all maintain stud books, register cats, and verify pedigrees. Most of them also charter clubs, sanction shows, and present awards.

Cat Show Organization

Although cat shows originated in Great Britain, the ones held there today are quite different from the ones in the United States. In Great Britain, judges go from cage to cage examining cats; during some judging, they even ask owners to leave the show hall. In the United States, however, judging takes place on *judging tables* set up in one area of the show hall in full view of all spectators and exhibitors attending. Behind each judging table is a row of cages, where cats entered in the same category are called to await judging. This setup of tables and cages is called a *judging ring.*

A single exhibition may have four or more judging rings set up, each operating as a separate competition and presided over by a different judge. Sometimes, separate clubs present back-to-back shows consisting of eight to ten rings over a two-day weekend. Cats can compete in all rings for which they are eligible. In the ring, the judge removes each cat from its cage, places it on the judging table in view of the audience, and thoroughly examines it. After evaluating all cats in the ring, the judge awards at least first-, second-, and third-place ribbons to the winners. All pedigreed cats are judged according to how closely they meet the written standard of perfection for their particular breed, pattern, and color.

All-Breed and Specialty Shows

If the show is an *all-breed* show, all cats, regardless of their type, compete against each other. *Specialty* shows, on the other hand, may be restricted to specific breeds or breed groups. Most commonly, specialty shows are restricted to the longhaired or shorthaired breeds. Depending on the association sponsoring the show, various divisions and classes exist for eligible pedigreed cats, altered cats, kittens, household pets, and new or experimental breeds and colors. Generally, unaltered, adult pedigreed cats begin their show careers competing in *open* classes against others of their breed, sex, and color. After achieving a specified number of wins, they become champions and can compete against other champions for the coveted title of grand champion. Many associations award additional titles beyond these.

Kittens and Household Pets

Pedigreed kittens between four and eight (or in some associations, ten) months of age can compete in classes with other kittens of their breed. The household pet (HHP) competition is for mixed-breed or nonpedigreed cats, which

must be spayed or neutered. Policies vary, but some associations permit a purebred cat to be shown as a household pet, as long as the owner surrenders the papers or does not register the cat as a purebred. Household pets are judged for their beauty, personality, and overall condition, rather than against a formal, written breed standard.

New Breeds and Colors

Practices for accepting and showing new or experimental breeds, colors, and varieties differ among the associations, but most allow such newcomers to be exhibited in nonchampionship classes. Depending on the association sponsoring the show, these classes may be labeled as Provisional, Miscellaneous, NBC (New Breeds and Colors), or AOV (Any Other Variety) classes.

In general, new breeds are exhibited first in noncompetitive, miscellaneous, NBC, or AOV classes before being granted prechampionship, or provisional breed, status. Cats in provisional breed competition are judged according to a provisional standard, but once their new breed gains full recognition, they become eligible for championship classes. While the Ragdoll can compete in championship classes in ACFA, ACA, CFF, TICA, AACE, CCA, NCFA, and UFO, the breed currently holds provisional standing in CFA. Ragdoll fanciers will be eligible to apply for championship status for their breed in this association in 1999.

Getting Ready to Show

If your dream is to exhibit your Ragdoll at cat shows, you will definitely want to purchase a show-quality animal. However, many breeders are understandably reluctant to sell a *top-show* quality kitten to a novice. It may be easier, and less expensive, for you to find a nice adult cat that has been retired from a breeding program or show career. In such cases, breeders typically alter these retired adults before placing them in good homes.

Alter classes, called *premiership* in the CFA, allow spayed and neutered pedigreed cats to compete against other altered cats of the same breed. Altered cats are judged according to the same standards as whole or intact cats, but instead of qualifying as a champion or grand champion, they earn comparable titles of *premier* or *grand premier* in the CFA. Many novice exhibitors prefer to show in alter classes, because acquiring and owning a show-alter cat affords an opportunity to compete on equal footing with breeders who've been in the business for years. Yet, having a show-alter relieves newcomers to the cat fancy of the extra commitment involved in keeping a breeding animal. So, if you want to show your Ragdoll, but you have no interest in breeding it, showing in premier or alter classes may be the best route to go.

Where to Start

First, find out about any upcoming shows that are going to be held near you. Check listings in the cat fanciers' magazines. The cat-registering associations also can provide information about affiliated cat shows and clubs in your area. Another good way to become involved in showing cats is to join a cat club in your area that is affiliated with one of the cat-registering associations. Many of these clubs organize and put on annual shows in their area (see Information on page 92).

Entry forms: After you decide what show you want to enter, contact the entry clerk for forms. Complete the entry forms and return them with the appropriate fees. The show flyer the clerk sends you will list all pertinent information about the show, including the cage dimensions.

Benching Cages

Benching cages for a single cat are small—usually about 2 feet wide by 2 feet high by 2 feet deep (61 × 61 × 61 cm). But for a little extra money, you may have the option of requesting a double cage on the entry form you submit. Usually, there is a place on the entry form where you can request to be *benched* next to someone you know. Your *benching assignment* is the cage where your cat will stay when it is not being judged in one of the rings. If your breeder, or someone you know who is an experienced exhibitor, will be exhibiting at the show, ask to be placed next to them. If you don't know anyone else who will be at the show, you may simply ask to be benched near other Ragdoll exhibitors.

Show Supplies and Preparations

After you return your forms and pay the appropriate entry fees, all you have to do is to get your cat ready and presentable for the show date. On the day of the show, you will need to bring some spray disinfectant to wipe down your cat's cage, plus fabric, towels, or show curtains to line the inside and bottom of the cage. Covering the cage gives your cat a little privacy amid the show hall noise and shields it from seeing the other cats in adjacent cages. This also adds an element of fun,

Seal bicolor Ragdoll.

because many shows have contests for the best-decorated cage.

Generally, the show committee provides a chair at each cage, cat litter, and sometimes disposable litter boxes. You'll have to bring a small litter pan, just in case, plus your grooming equipment, a grooming table (a sturdy TV tray or plastic patio table serve the same purpose), a cat carrier, a cat bed, food and water bowls, your cat's favorite food, and any other accessories to make your cat feel comfortable.

Of course, you will have completed most of your Ragdoll's grooming at home, having bathed it a day or two before the show and having made sure that your cat has no sign

Seal point bicolor.

of fleas. Only touch-ups should be required at the show, but be prepared and take all your grooming supplies with you, including a battery-powered blow dryer, just in case your cat makes a major mess of its fur in transit.

Transport your Ragdoll in its carrier and take along a pet bed, a favorite toy, feeding bowls, food, and medications. It's also a good idea to take a gallon or two of water from home, or bottled water, because different drinking water can sometimes bring on a bout of diarrhea.

The show flyer should recommend hotels that allow pets. If not, ask in advance about the pet policy at the place where you plan to stay, and don't forget to take a litter box for use in the hotel room.

The Day of the Show

When the big day arrives, check in early at the door and get your cat settled in its assigned cage. Read the catalog schedule to determine when your cat will be judged. Also, note the number for your entry in the catalog, as this is how your cat will be called to the ring. Once the show starts, keep your ear tuned to the public address system. When you hear your cat's number called, carry your cat to the appropriate judging ring. Your number will be posted on top of one of the cages in the ring. Place your cat in the correct cage, then take a seat in the audience to quietly watch the judging.

Judging

The judge will examine each cat in turn on the table and hang ribbons on the winners' cages at the end of the class. When the judging is over, the clerk will ask the exhibitors to remove their cats from the ring. Collect your cat and ribbons, if any, and return to your benching cage to await your call to the next ring. Depending on how well your cat does, it may be called back for finals, when the top contestants in a given category are presented. The highest awards at a show include Best of Breed and the most coveted prize, Best in Show. Cats that win in the championship or premiership finals earn points based on the number of cats defeated at the show. These points count toward regional and national titles. To understand the ribbons, points, and awards system more fully, consult the rules booklet prepared by the cat fancy association sponsoring the show.

Ragdoll Breed Standard

A cat show is not simply a beauty contest, although grooming and appearance are extremely important. Every pedigreed cat competing in a show is judged according to how well it meets the written standard for its particular breed. A breed standard is a written blueprint describing the ideal conformation and coloring of animals representing that breed. The standard describes in detail how the head, body, coat, and color should appear in the ideal specimen. To successfully show cats, you must be familiar with the breed standard accepted by the association(s) sponsoring the shows in which you exhibit.

The breed standard also dictates the goals of a professional breeding program. For use in their breeding programs, conscientious breeders try to select cats that most closely fit the standard or that possess enough of the desired qualities outlined in the standard to promise outstanding offspring. Ideally, their aim is to breed the best to the best whenever possible.

From time to time, breed standards may be revised or rewritten by formal committees that convene periodically to amend and update them. This is due to the fact that selective breeding sometimes results in new colors or varieties that need to be added to the standard after meeting certain criteria for acceptance. Breed standards may also change on occasion because the favored look of the breed evolves and changes over time.

The Ragdoll Fanciers Club International has a general breed standard for the Ragdoll cat, but each cat-registering association also has its own version. While breed standards can vary among the different cat associations, as well as from country to country, the Ragdoll standard is relatively consistent. Practices for accepting new colors and varieties can vary widely, too, and some associations or countries may recognize colors not currently accepted elsewhere. So, if you're planning to enter a show, be sure to acquaint yourself with the breed standard and rules of the association that is sponsoring that show. For more information on standards, write to the appropriate association(s) (see page 92).

Boarding Your Ragdoll

If you're taking one cat to a show but leaving another at home, ask a trusted friend or neighbor to look in on it, or consider hiring a pet sitter to care for it while you're away. Leaving your Ragdoll in its normal environment is less traumatic than boarding it in unfamiliar surroundings at a kennel or a veterinarian's office. However, deviation from the normal household routine upsets some animals and may result in behavior problems, such as house-soiling. If your Ragdoll is subject to this behavior, it may be better off at a boarding facility, where it can be supervised. To lessen your Ragdoll's separation anxiety, leave something with your scent on it to comfort the cat while you're away.

If you decide to use a professional pet-sitter or boarding kennel, ask friends for recommendations, and check out the operator's references and business credentials. Inspect a boarding facility's premises for cleanliness beforehand, and ask about provisions for your cat's security and comfort. Select a kennel that houses cats in an area separate from dogs. A reputable kennel will require pets to be free of fleas and will also ask for proof that animals are up to date on all inoculations.

Whatever arrangements you choose to make, leave an itinerary of where you will be and how you can be reached. Also, be sure to leave your veterinarian's telephone number with the person tending to your cat.

Even if you're going away for several hours and leave out enough food and water in self-feeders for your cat, let someone know where you're going and when you'll be back. That someone should also have a key to your home and permission to enter and look after your cat in case you are delayed.

An Owner's Responsibility

Regardless of whether you want a Ragdoll to show or simply as a treasured companion, remember that your conscientiousness as a cat owner will inevitably be noticed by others. In this way, you have an opportunity to demonstrate to others by your own caring actions how to properly tend to a feline companion. Many cat owners take this responsibility seriously and strive to become the best educated pet owners they can be. They visit shows, attend pet care seminars, participate in clubs, and read books and magazines about cats. Some even volunteer to serve and support their local humane shelters, helping to improve the plight and existence of all cats, not just purebred ones.

Such an attitude is admirable, because the Ragdoll kitten you acquire and raise to adulthood represents a significant financial and emotional investment on your part, as well as on the part of your breeder. The more strongly you communicate the value of this investment to others, the more likely you are to instill a similar appreciation in others regarding your chosen breed, and about cats in general. In this way, you can make a difference by enlightening others and by simply helping to raise their awareness of what it really means to be a responsible and caring pet owner.

Photo Credits

Chanan Photography: pages 4, 8, 9, 12, 16, 21, 32, 33, 41, 45, 48, 52, 56, 57, 68, 76, 89, 92; Tara Darling: pages 2–3, 17, 20, 44, 49, 81; Susan Green: pages 24, 28, 29, 33, 36, 40, 60, 69, 72, 73, 80; Mark McCullough: pages 8, 16, 48, 64, 88; Paws for Pictures: page 84.

Cover Photos

Chanan Photography: back cover and inside back cover; Tara Darling: inside front cover; Mark McCullough: front cover.

Important Note

This pet owner's guide tells the reader how to buy and care for a Ragdoll Cat. The author and the publisher consider it important to point out that the advice given in the book is meant primarily for normally developed kittens from a reputable breeder; that is, cats of excellent physical health and good temperament.

Anyone who adopts a fully grown Ragdoll Cat should be aware that the animal has already formed its basic impressions of human beings. The new owner should watch the cat carefully, including its behavior toward humans, and should meet the previous owner. If the cat comes from a shelter, it may be possible to get some information on its background and peculiarities.

When you handle cats, you may get scratched or bitten. If this happens, have a doctor treat the injuries immediately.

Make sure your cat receives all the necessary immunizations and wormings. Otherwise, its health may be endangered, and it could even pass on some diseases to humans. If your cat shows signs of illness, consult the veterinarian and call your doctor if you are worried about your own health.

Some people have allergic reactions to cat hair. If you think you might be allergic, ask your doctor before you get a cat.

© Copyright 1999 by Karen Leigh Davis.

All inquiries should be addressed to:
Barron's Educational Series, Inc.
250 Wireless Boulevard
Hauppauge, NY 11788
http://www.barronseduc.com

Library of Congress Catalog Card No. 98-33446

ISBN-13: 978-0-7641-0732-0
ISBN-10: 0-7641-0732-1

Library of Congress Cataloging-in-Publicaton Data
Davis, Karen Leigh, 1953–
    Ragdoll cats : everything about purchase, care, nutrition, health care, behavior, and showing / Karen Leigh Davis.
        p.   cm. — (A complete pet owner's manual)
        Includes bibliographical references (p.   ) and index.
        ISBN 0-7641-0732-1
        1. Ragdoll cat. I. Title. II. Series.
    SF449.R34D28   1999
    636.8'3—dc21   98-33446
                                                      CIP

Printed in China
9 8 7 6 5

All Ragdolls have dark-colored markings, which are called points. Faint color markings on the ears, face, legs, and tail become visible when a kitten is a few weeks old and darken with maturity, as seen in the serene Ragdoll pictured here.